THE GREAT PEACE

THE GREAT PEACE

AN ASIAN'S CANDID REPORT
ON RED CHINA

By RAJA HUTHEESING

HARPER & BROTHERS PUBLISHERS NEW YORK

Library of Congress catalog card number: 53–7736

CONTENTS

All autocratic rulers mislead when they say they unify the people. This is impossible. They do not rule the people with gentleness but steal the people's right to liberty and make them afraid. What is called the Great Peace in an autocracy always contains in it the seeds of decay.

MONTESQUIEU

Part One

JOURNEY
TO THE WALLED CITY

1

CONDUCTED TOUR

"Those who speak know nothing.
Those who know are silent."
These words, as I am told,
Were spoken by Lao-tzŭ.
If we are to believe that Lao-tzŭ
    Was himself *one who knew*,
How comes it that he wrote a book
    Of five thousand words?

                Po Chü-i

THE invitation to go to China on behalf of the India-China Friendship Association came early in September, 1951. After many years of active participation in our struggle for freedom as a member of the Indian National Congress, I had left politics for journalism. I felt the frustration and despair of the Indian people who had hoped that free India would fight against misrule, oppression and poverty. But our leadership had been found wanting and millions continued to live without hope in hunger and ignorance. China seemed to offer a new way by which the Asian people

3

could acquire the means of improving their lot. I was eager to see for myself the achievements of the Chinese people.

I had waited for this opportunity for many years. My association with China had begun in 1937, when, as Secretary to the China Aid Committee of the Indian National Congress, I had helped to organize a medical unit to go to Chunking as a token of our sympathy with the Chinese people in their struggle against Japanese aggression. Since then, I had read everything about China I could get hold of. Writers like Edgar Snow, Epstein and Gunther Stein had praised Mao Tse-tung and his achievements at Yenan. They had said that the Communist Party of China cared little for dogma and in fact acted as "liberal land reformers" in order to unify the country and provide it with a progressive administration. Imperialism and corruption had oppressed the Chinese people for centuries and many problems which they face today are similar to what we in India and other underdeveloped countries of Asia face.

Hunger, ignorance, want and misery had made the life of the Chinese cheap and tawdry, yet they had kept their gentle smile and their love of peace. For two thousand years India and China had lived as peaceful neighbors following many common pursuits in co-operation and mutual understanding. We had learned much from each other of art, religion, philosophy and literature. Centuries ago, travelers had crossed the Himalayas and the Central Asian deserts to draw inspiration and strength from one another and had left their imprint behind at Taxshila, Lung-men and Tatung. Today, with the overthrow of Chiang Kai-shek, China is united and vast changes have taken place under the determined leadership of Mao Tse-tung and the Communist Party. The Communists in India claimed that the standard of living of the Chinese people was improving daily; that the great river valley projects had been completed ahead of schedule by the sheer determination of millions who joyfully worked for the nation; that education, housing and medical care were rapidly improving while India floundered in food shortages and cloth rationing.

The Communists insist that in the People's Democracy there are no concentration camps, no subjugation of the people's will by fear, no suppression of the liberties of the individual. They claim there is democracy for the people and dictatorship only over the evils of corruption, imperialistic exploitation and reaction. China, they say, provides all the answers to men who believe in national freedom, individual liberty and the right to food, shelter, clothing and equal opportunity. I did not want to question this *fang-shen* or renewal of the body, which many propagandists claimed was going on in China. It is for the Chinese to decide what is good for them. The Indians would only be too glad if our neighbor and ancient colleague had found the means of achieving the happiness of her people and, I thought, I might learn much of help to my country if I went there.

So I readily accepted the opportunity to visit China for six weeks in October and November, 1951, on behalf of the India-China Friendship Association as a guest of various Chinese groups. Before I left I made arrangements with the Press Trust of India to send them reports for publication in Indian newspapers. Our itinerary included a stay of two weeks in Peking on the occasion of the second anniversary of the People's Democracy on October 1, 1951. Then we visited Mukden, Tientsin, Nanking, Shanghai and Canton, so that we might see for ourselves the agricultural and industrial achievements of new China. The trip also included a visit to villages under land reform and to Hangchow, a health resort. After six weeks, I returned home.

As we traveled from one city to another and went to institutions, industrial plants and official receptions, we listened to speeches telling us of various achievements under the leadership of the Communist Party since the liberation of the country. District officers, managers of industry, government officials and ministers monotonously repeated as facts what proved in reality to be propaganda claims. Newspapers, magazines and books all followed set formulas and there were no differences of opinion, no contradictions, nothing which could admit of possible alternatives. Everything was a ritual meticulously carried out to display the theoretical achievements of publicized targets. I, a visitor, moved as an automaton directed about to see and to understand only that which redounded to the glory of a totalitarian state. I realized that communism was the new god of China, the Holy Dragon.

Deep the waters of the Black Pool, coloured like ink,
They say a Holy Dragon lives there whom men have never
    seen,
Beside the pool they have built a shrine; the authorities have
    established a ritual,
A dragon by itself remains a dragon, but men can make it
    a god.

                                                    Po Chü-i

Once back in India, it was difficult to disentangle the facts from fiction while the numerous impressions of six weeks crowded into my mind. I was anxious to return, if I could, without the obligations of a guest to his host, and find confirmation or contradiction. I knew the Press Trust of India was anxious to establish a permanent representative in Peking, so that Indian newspapers could be supplied with news on China. The government of India also wanted an independent news service to function from China, as they believed it would promote a better understanding between the peoples of the two countries. I therefore spoke little on China, knowing that any expression of views on my part would close the doors of China against me.

In March, 1952, the government of India announced that an official Cultural Delegation was to visit China on the occasion of the May Day celebrations. When the Press Trust asked me if I was willing to go as a newsman and develop their contact with China once again, I seized the opportunity. My first itinerary in China was extended by a visit to the Huai River project and to the cultural relics of Tatung and the Confucius Temple.

I returned to China as a journalist. I knew the difficulties of traveling about and finding living accommodations as a private visitor. I had to have an identity card to move about, needed permits to travel and secure quarters and required facilities to change money. I therefore asked the assistance of the External Affairs Ministry in requesting the Indian Ambassador at Peking, Mr. Panikkar, to obtain these for me before I accepted the assignment. Because the Chinese were willing to welcome me, I was told that all the preparations would be made. Nonetheless, I left India with many misgivings, for I knew the Chinese really welcomed only Communist journalists.

I was perturbed as well because a personal note I had written to the Prime Minister about conditions in China had been circulated to the members of the Indian Delegation by the Ministry through a careless secretary. The note had indicated there was little economic progress in China despite the claims of exportable food surplus. If it fell into Chinese hands, I knew I would be placed in an awkward situation. I asked the Ministry to withdraw the note, but it was too late.

An incident at Canton on arrival created further difficulties. One of the delegates wanted to photograph a poor Chinese child carrying a younger child on its back, and asked me to help pose the children. When he had snapped his picture, I began to take one too, and was suddenly interrupted by the interpreter who covered the lens of my camera. The next morning I was informed by the Secretary of the Delegation that the Chinese had complained I was trying to photograph "restricted areas." I was surprised, and offered to hand over my film; but was merely told that as a foreign correspondent I had to obtain a permit to use my camera. The incident, I thought, ended there as far as the Chinese were concerned.

On arrival at Peking, I inquired about my accreditation papers from the Embassy officials. I was told I had only to sign some papers and wait half an hour or so for my card. I did not know then that I would have to wait seven days for it because the Indian Ambassador, Mr. Panikkar, had decided that I was an "undesirable person."

Mr. Panikkar is a short, heavy man with a goatee, whose eyes twinkle with self-conscious pleasure at his own remarks. He is a quick, clever conversationalist who has been described as an "intellectual hedgehog with every spine erect and quivering with ideas." For many years he served the Indian maharajas and acquired the habit of mind which wants to please the powers that be at all times, and by now is everything to all men and believes only in himself. Nehru once said, "He will be Communist in Peking and a champion of freedom in Washington so long as it takes Mr. Panikkar somewhere." In Chiang Kai-shek's China he was a believer in Kuomintang invincibility and from Nanking advised the government of India to enter into a defense pact with Chiang in 1948. When I met him in Peking in October, 1951, after a lapse of many years, I listened to his discourses on the achievements of the New Democracy only to find that all his "facts" were Chinese Communist propaganda.

When I came to Peking on my second visit, I was a journalist known to have opposed the Congress Party during the Indian elections, and in my note on China I had dared to contradict Mr. Panikkar's views. He had therefore decided to prevent me from carrying out my duties as a journalist. For a full week I stayed at one of the small houses of the Indian Embassy sharing a room with a friend, without food, without money, without any permit that would enable me to move about the city, until I cabled to the Press Trust of India and sought the intervention of the External Affairs Ministry in order to obtain my accreditation.

During this "imprisonment" I was kept in the dark about the reasons for the difficulties. Mr. Panikkar had said the Chinese had secured my note and thought it cause for objection. I later learned that he had complained of my views on China to the Indian Delegation and denied having received any instructions about me from the Ministry. To the Ministry, in turn, he had reported the photograph incident at Canton. When the Ministry requested further explanations, he said he was trying to get my personal status—not my journalistic standing—recognized by the Chinese.

When, at last, accreditation was obtained, a new sort of censorship inhibited me. I was told the Indian Embassy had had to assure the Chinese that I would not send out any reports detrimental to them, and that, therefore, all my dispatches would have to be cleared by the Embassy before being sent. I was further instructed that I could report only the activities of the Indian Delegation and not participate in question periods during their visits to various institutions. I learned, eventually, that these conditions had not been imposed by the Chinese at all, and once we left Peking I did as I chose.

Normally I would have asked my employers to recall me, but I was anxious to retrace my steps along what was now a familiar route. I had no desire to listen again to the monotonous official statements and was content, instead, to let my eyes wander and note the changes that had occurred between my two visits, and to bring some order into the many impressions I had gathered.

My first visit had taught me that any journey through China was a conducted tour, and all talks, meetings and contacts were possible only under the watchful eyes of the interpreters and through them, since the Chinese even when they knew English refused to speak it. I met many university professors who were graduates of British or American universities and knew English perfectly, yet consistently refused to talk in English or admit to understanding my questions until they were translated into Chinese. Often I received answers which could only be explained on the grounds of an incorrect translation by the interpreters, whose knowledge of English was limited; for even when the person questioned understood me his reply was dictated by the poor translation put before him.

Mme. Sun Yat-sen, who had been educated in the United States, would not talk in English at first because, she said, she had forgotten it. Mrs. Pandit, the leader of the Indian Delegation, had to talk to her through an interpreter. We first met Mme. Sun in October, 1951. She looked her age and had put on weight. I had heard that once upon a time she was a beautiful woman. She still has charm and a distinguished appearance. She refuses to wear the blue uniform of the Chinese Communists and each time I saw her at various receptions in October, 1951, and again in Shanghai in May, 1952, she was dressed smartly in black. Her hair, which still appeared to be black, was tightly drawn back in a bun at the back of her head. There was something frail and fragile about her walk and, throughout a rather superficial and formal interview, her eyes looked wistfully sad. Perhaps the first enthusiasm of her comradeship with the Communists had worn off. Though the Communists now pay occasional tribute to Sun Yat-sen, they do not approve of giving him much importance. Unfortunately our conversation was limited to inviting her to India for she sidestepped any discussion on the grounds of being unable to speak due to a bad cold. Though our talk had begun through an interpreter she gradually drifted into slow but perfectly spoken English.

Mme. Kung Pen, the director of Information and Research in the Foreign Ministry, also speaks perfect English. She cross-examined me for ten minutes at the Germ Warfare Exhibition Press Conference, for she was anxious to find out my reactions to the exhibition, but she refused to speak in English when two members of the Indian Cultural

Delegation went to see her at the Foreign Office in order to obtain some information on China.

A journalist colleague had defended this unwillingness to speak English as a matter of national pride and policy. I should have thought that it would be a matter of courtesy to the guests to speak to them in a language they understood. The Indian visitors to China were on a good will mission and were not engaged in diplomatic negotiations which require linguistic exactitude. It is a matter of policy with the Communists, and I believe it is common to all Communist countries, that no conversation is permitted which is not checked and double-checked by a colleague. Under such scrutiny, all conversation, talks and information supplied become monotonously repetitious and add little to the knowledge of the visitor. All "facts," statistics and descriptions are duly repeated, often from a written script. The story is told again and again till the visitor, like the Chinese people, believes it as truth proved by all available evidence. It is not strange that many honest and well-meaning people have come back from China and reported these stories as their observations.

If we disbelieved what we were told, it may be said, what of the evidence of our eyes? Many of us who have visited China are constantly invited to tell of our experiences. Yet what could we have seen except what we were shown? It has been said that the visitor to China is conducted only to the extent that a program is arranged for him which he is free to follow or not. But no visit to any place in China is possible without prearrangements. It is impossible for any visitor to go where he chooses though he may decline to go where the program expects him to go. It is not only the language difficulty which gets in the way.

CONDUCTED TOUR

A member of the Indian Delegation one day decided not to accompany the Delegation but to go instead to call on one of the foreign professors at Peking University to whom he had a letter of introduction. As it happened, the interpreter who would normally have accompanied him had gone with the Delegation. When he arrived at the university, he wandered about with the piece of paper bearing the professor's name in his hands asking people to take him to the professor. No one he met would conduct him there. After a while someone who spoke English turned up at his side and gently reminded him that it was not possible for him to see the professor or the university unless it had been arranged. The delegate went back to the hotel, unable to see his friend. Later he was quietly informed that he should not have gone to the university, which is a restricted area, unaccompanied by the interpreter.

It is true that the guests were asked their preferences and interests. When arrangements could be made, the visitor was taken there. Otherwise he was likely to be told that no such place or institution existed. During my first visit to Nanking, I had seen an exhibition arranged by Nanking University. Among the exhibits was the charter given to an American Mission permitting the founding of the university. This sought to prove that American "imperialism" had planned to degrade the Chinese culture. English textbooks which were merely books on politics and economics were displayed with passages marked in red pencil to convince the visitor that there was a plan to denationalize the Chinese student. I knew that millions of American dollars had gone into this university. I therefore suggested to the Indian Delegation, on my second visit, that they ask the Chinese to include a visit to this university, because some of the members were leading educators in India. When the Secretary to the Delegation made the request, he was informed that no such university existed in Nanking! Apparently it was a lapse of memory. Ultimately a visit was arranged, but for only one member of the Delegation who was able to meet only one or two professors and see a few students at work.

There are innumerable such instances and to repeat them would be monotonous. I know I may be charged with stating what many others have denied. It may be that these others feel it would be discourteous to our hosts to say that facilities were not given us to see all that we wished. I feel, however, that we owe our people the truth, especially when our courteous acknowledgments are being used as facts to undermine our freedom and democracy in India, and to prove that progress lies in the Communist way.

Despite the limited activity permitted the visitor, a vivid but fleeting impression occasionally highlights one thing or another and we succeed in getting a perspective. Such a perspective, coupled with some familiarity with the economic and industrial development of China in the past, helps us to understand what has been happening in recent years. Above all what is needed is an objective mind which seeks the reality through the mass of propaganda, refusing to accept or reject until proof is obtained.

The task of knowing the reality is somewhat easier in China because she has not yet grown adept in the methods of communism. Vast multitudes are preoccupied with the problems of daily bread, while the country has still to be organized into a cohesive whole. Today, though China is unified and the writ of Peking runs from Mukden to Canton and Sian to Shanghai, she has still to evolve an administration which will fasten its totalitarian grip completely on the life of the people. "Liberation" is a recent achievement, while the problems which she faces are old and of gigantic proportions. I listened for overtones, undertones and subtle changes of words by repeating my questions to as many people as I could. My reiterated questionings, though they earned me many scowls and discourtesies from the officers in charge of the visitors, brought me such interesting statements as, "the Russians took away all the machinery from Manchuria and returned very little" and, "the North Koreans were impatient."

I also had the advantage of repeating my visit after a short interval. I was thus able to check the claims of progress and compare conditions at two different periods. My political experience and economic training as the Secretary to the National Planning Committee in India during the years 1939–1942 had given me sufficient understanding of the implications of economic progress in underdeveloped countries. I know that the primary urges of oppressed and hungry people are freedom, national and individual, and the right to live as human beings with adequate food, shelter and clothing. I have seen these urges drive the frustrated people of Asia and Africa toward communism for their satisfaction.

I have always had great admiration for the Chinese people. I am conscious that the Chinese people's struggle for freedom and peace is a part of our common struggle and our aims could be better realized by friendship for and understanding of each other. But I am also convinced that totalitarian rule enslaves and endangers peace and progress. This would perhaps have been none of our concern if the Chinese people were content with Communist rule, and we could continue to live in friendship and co-operation. I have tried to put down what I have seen only because international communism seeks to disrupt the freedom of the Asian countries by painting false pictures of China and thus rousing men, hungry for food and shelter, against their own people.

During the general elections in India I saw how the Communist claims affected the Indian voter. Many colleagues who were with me on my first trip to China were fellow travelers of the Communists who praised all we saw. The traditional sympathy and friendship between China and India strengthened such propaganda and influenced the people. Most members of the Indian Cultural Delegation were silent from considerations of courtesy. These claims of progress, therefore, continue to affect millions in Asia who are unaware that in the name of freedom, peace and progress, they are being slowly led to accept the principles of a totalitarian dictatorship which will deny the very things they seek.

I realize I have only touched the fringes of a vast country and saw only what the Chinese considered was "for view." My observations may be overreaching and unjustified. But what little I did see must be shared with those who in their earnestness to better the lot of the common man might otherwise labor in a cause that will undermine our national freedom and democracy.

Under Gandhi I had learned the importance of rightful means but I am not obsessed by its philosophy. I know it is foolish to ask hungry people to wait till proper means are found to obtain their needs. Yet what I have seen in China convinces me that evil means lead to success, if at all, only for a while. These means have within them the seeds of destruction of the very ends they seek to achieve.

I went to China to see whether the Chinese people have won freedom and democracy under the New Democratic Dictatorship of Mao Tse-tung. I found a government waging a ruthless class war.

I went to China to see how progress was made possible under communism. I know communism is a faith which claims to be the only true knowledge and denies all questionings as mere heresies. Faith is nurtured on miracles and the Communists claim many miracles of economic, cultural and scientific progress. I believe progress is possible only when men's minds are free to question, fearless to dare and open to doubt.

I found industrial stagnation for want of technical knowhow. The few technical men that China has were being persecuted and put through a process of brainwashing or "reform through labor."

I saw that land reform had brought satisfaction to the peasants and peacetime agriculture had led to normal returns. But the peasants' passions were now being used to further the aims and objects of a Communist dictatorship.

An ancient Taoist discourse offers a moral for today:

Hui Tzu said to Chuang Tzu: "Can a man really become passionless?"

Chuang Tzu said: "He can."

Hui Tzu said: "A man without passions cannot be called a man."

Chuang Tzu said: "Tao gave him substance; Heaven gave him form; how is it possible not to call him a man?"

Hui Tzu said: "I would rather say, granted that he is still a man, how is it possible for him to be passionless?"

17

THE GREAT PEACE

Chuang Tzu said: "You do not understand what I mean. When I say passionless I mean that a man does not let love or hate do him damage within and that he falls in with the way in which things happen of themselves and does not exploit life."

Hui Tzu said: "If he does not exploit life, what is the use of his having a body?"*

I saw a great people roused into life by a new hope but only for a while. Now they are again caught in the gathering winds of darkness which seek to crush the passions of their nation: its humanity, gentleness, tolerance and love of knowledge. The four hundred millions of China are being reduced to mere passionless bodies in the service of a dictatorship, for they have bartered their humanity for their right to eat.

* "Chuang Tzu," translated by Arthur Waley.

2

PEKING

TRAVELING in China as an honored guest of the government can be a pleasant experience. There are no air services unless the government puts an army plane at the disposal of the guest. But the trains are clean and punctual, and the guests have special railway coaches to themselves. There is none of the hustle and bustle of railroad stations in democratic countries, and the few passengers who have obtained the privilege of moving from one place to another are kept quiet and orderly.

On my first visit I entered China from Hongkong by a few hours' journey to Canton. There were no direct trains and we had to walk for about a furlong at the customs barrier. I saw, then, how well guarded the frontiers were. The Chinese traveler had to go through a thorough screening before he was allowed in. There were repeated examinations of his luggage on the train by armed guards who carried sten guns. Propaganda speeches were made and literature was sold on the train by youth leaguers, and every station had armed soldiers to keep watch.

We were greeted at the Canton station by large numbers

of boys and girls with flowers in their hands, lined up to give us a gala welcome. Beyond them in a row stood representatives of numerous public organizations. Shaking hands with them we moved out and were quickly hustled into cars to be driven away to the guesthouse. There the local hosts received us. We were individually introduced and served with tea and fruits, while we waited for rooms to be allotted to us. In the evening there was a banquet where speeches of welcome were delivered and we replied to them expressing the good will and friendship of the Indian people for the Chinese people. This was the inevitable routine which followed us wherever we went.

That evening, I was reminded I was in war-weary China. I was dressing for dinner after a quick bath when the air raid sirens went off and the whole city was wrapped in darkness. I could not understand why these air raid precaution measures were being taken and against whom. Later when I inquired nobody could offer any explanation except that Formosa was not far away and Chiang's agents were most active in the South. During a stay of some four days in Canton we experienced these precautions three times. They seemed to be a normal routine.

Canton is one big bazaar. Every street was a continuing series of shops full of odd goods which must have come out of old hoardings. There were few shoppers except in the government department stores. The streets are jarringly ugly with the names of the shops in big Chinese letters providing the only decoration. There was no traffic except a few pedicabs; and hundreds of these cycle-driven rickshaws with their faded red covers waited alongside the road for business. Our cars went down these roads at a tearing speed hooting their electric horns ceaselessly.

PEKING

Along the Pearl River and on the canals lived thousands of families in junks. One morning I walked down the riverside road, watching these families living their lives with little privacy. It was a colorful sight. There were more beautiful women and children in these little junks on the Pearl than all the women I have seen in the rest of China. In their simple, tight-fitting, short blue or black dresses, combing their long, glistening black hair, with their almond-skinned faces with a slight pink flush, they provided a sight which I cannot forget. It is a pity that they were beginning to lose their smiles and appear grim and stern in short-cut hair and crumpled Sun Yat-sen suits.

In the heart of the city stands the ruin of an old building, an empty shell with its colonnade of pillars dominating the modern exhibition grounds. It is a reminder of the sufferings of the Chinese people and the long struggle against the Japanese. At another corner, across the bridge which connects the old British concession with the city, stands another memorial, a memorial of the "Shakee Massacre" when British and French troops fired on demonstrators.

Today soldiers of the People's Liberation Army patrol this bridge. I saw a Chinese porter walking on it with a bundle on his head. A soldier with a gun slung across his shoulder was lazily watching the porter, and as he came near, he pushed his gun across the path. "Where is your card?" the soldier demanded. Quietly the poor man put down his load by the side of the road and dug into his pockets to pull out a red identity card. This was the New China.

From Canton we flew to Peking via Hankow. It was a Dakota plane and it took us eight hours to reach our destination. The airports at Canton and Hankow were in terrible condition. The air strips were full of potholes and there was no place to sit down and wait. But the flight over the great Yangtze was a wonderful sight. The vast expanse of water showed the river overflowing its banks, and for miles around every bit of land was cultivated. Terrace farming was not unknown in China. As we flew over, I was reminded of the traditions of hard work which the Chinese peasantry had put into the land. I had heard somewhere that the Chinese peasant considered himself to be the middleman between heaven and earth. Floods and famines he took as his daily fate and he worked on tirelessly on the land he loved so dearly.

And so to Peking, the imperial city with its ancient wall, yellow-tiled roofs of the Manchus and beautiful palaces. Peking is the most typical Chinese town which has endured many dynasties. Jacaranda and laburnum trees line its wide main street along the eastern wall of the Forbidden City. The Tien An Man, "The Gate of Heavenly Peace," appears to be a ready-made Red Square. With its imposing East Gate, red-lacquered pillars, yellow-tiled roof and red silk ballooned Chinese lamps, it dominates the life of New China. It was in this square two years ago that Mao Tse-tung declared from the high balcony of the gate across the six white marbled bridges which lead into the Forbidden City: "The People's Government of China today assumes power in Peking." I saw in this square two years later, on October 1, 1951, the people's assembled might, as the Liberation Army marched along equipped with American armaments captured from the Kuomintang troops. The parade lasted six hours and was accompanied by all the usual paraphernalia which Moscow uses: flags, huge pictures, flowers and dancers.

PEKING

Edgar Snow describes Peking as a city where something had to happen. He writes in *Battle for Asia:*

[Peking] was an anomaly whose days were numbered, a medieval survival where over a million men dwelt among the glitter and loot of centuries accumulated within its wonderful maze of walls . . . Peking was a city of retired courtiers and soldiers of empire, of scholars and absentee landlords, of monks and artisan merchants and of ricksha coolies speaking a cultured tongue; a city nobly conceived and nobly made, a treasury of art, a place of gentle birth and of decadence, of diplomatic intrigues over rapturous food, of more charm than character, and of more knavery than downright wickedness; a city of warm vivid springs and shadowed autumns, and of winter sunshine sparkling on snow-covered trees and frozen lakes, a city of eternal compromise and easy laughter, of leisure and of family love; of poverty and tragedy, and indifference to dirt; and yet a place of unexpected violence, where regenerate students coined the fighting slogans of a nation, and blinding Mongolian storms swept down from the Gobi Desert, leaving the graceful temples and golden palace roofs strewn with the oldest dust of life.

And now something had happened to Peking. The dust had been swept clean and though the haunting beauty of the temples and the gleam of the palace roofs remained, there was no easy laughter. Art and gentle living had disappeared and their place was taken by grim humorless men and women in blue cotton uniforms to be molded to one pattern of life. The scholar too had left and the slogan-shouting peasant had replaced him. New Forbidden Cities had been built within the ancient walls. Only the rickshaw coolies remained, sitting and smoking as they waited for customers.

Peking had become clean, hard-working and disciplined. There were no regenerate students, only young men going through a strict course of brainwashing and reorientation. The famous eating places had disappeared for there were no more gourmets. I have never sat down to a worse meal than at the State Banquet in celebration of the Republic Day. I sensed the austere living, self-sacrifice and hunger.

The corridors of the Summer Palace and the Winter Palace are filled with plain-clothed peasants and district visitors who come to Peking to take part in the parades. There is no swish of silks and rich brocades. The common man has come into his own, they say. More likely he is in the Liberation Army which clustered every evening in the Tien An Man Square to dance and play till late in the evening. In the Park within the walls of the Forbidden City grow peonies. Few flowers in the world compare in beauty and fragrance. The Temple of Heaven, the lakes and the nine Dragon Walls gleamed in the autumn sunshine of Peking.

I remember one evening returning late from dinner with a French Sinologist and his charming wife. I took a pedi-cab home. It was a beautiful spring night and the driver was in a talkative mood. In his broken English he recounted to me stories of old Peking along the Embassy Row. He would point out a building and describe the foreigners who lived there in the days of the Empire. To-day, he wistfully remarked, some government offices had taken their place. He talked of banquets and wonderful cooking of bygone days. When he dropped me, I had no change to pay him, so I offered him a twenty-thousand-yuan bill. He laughed and said, "What could you do with the change I owe you!" I let it go at that.

Peking was China, and all the men who were shaping her future destiny were there. But for me it was a dull round of inconsequential banquets where the same speeches were repeated by the hosts and the guests. Good will and friendship, two-thousand-mile-long common frontier and two thousand years of interflow of culture between India and China, world peace and Asian unity, all came in with the usual platitudes while we talked through our interpreters to the famous names on our right and left and drank raw wine and harsh liquor. If one wanted to talk seriously, it was difficult to meet the Chinese singly for they were always too busy. A colleague hazarded to ask Chou En-lai some questions on land reform. It was suggested that he see the villages first, then come and talk with Chou. Of course the opportunity never came. For the visitor Peking proved only a sight-seeing tour where ancient monuments are mixed up in his impressions with official handouts delivered to him in lectures.

I stayed in Peking two weeks each time I went there. I saw Chinese opera specially performed for the visitors, heard the new music composed on the lines of the Russian revolutionary songs and saw the folk dances of the Minorities. Mei Lan-fang, the greatest Chinese actor, who plays the role of a woman to perfection, came out of retirement to dazzle us with his grace and charm. The swish of the beautiful silks and the clinging folds of the Chinese draperies now exist only on the stage. It was all work, work to build a nation of heroes; and out of this stern silence perhaps a new power will emerge which will hold men's lives for a paltry ransom.

I visited universities, listened to talks on land reform and inflation, passed a day among the villagers on the outskirts of Peking and talked to some of the foreign Embassies, but nothing stands out in my memory so vividly as the few hours I passed in Chi Pei-she's studio where he painted a picture at my request. That was the only ordinary Chinese home I or any other Indian ever entered in China. I had been to Kuo Mo-jo's home for a private interview and had tea at Mme. Sun Yat-sen's but these were official, formal calls. The newspapers told us nothing about the life of the people about us and we often felt completely alone and cut off from the millions who lived in Peking. I can well imagine the need to fill up the intellectual vacuum which many Chinese must feel. It was a fertile ground in which to sow ideas. Perhaps the Communists worked on the theory that the human mind will resist being confined for long to feed upon itself. It must ultimately relax its intellectual guards and accept whatever is available.

My two weeks in Peking in October, 1951, were completely planned out. There were daily visits to "places of interest." We were met by some authority in charge and after handshakes and mutual clappings we were led to a room where the inevitable tea and fruits were laid out. Then the chairman would get up and tell us about the institution, giving us some details and statistics of the percentage of progress between "before liberation" and "after liberation." Sometimes we would be allowed to ask questions or we would be informed that we could ask them after we had seen the place. After the tour, there would be tea and fruits again and a few questions. In the universities we seldom saw or met the students. Generally we were shown the library, or some scientific or historical exhibition arranged for the visitors.

We also had on our program visits to the various people's

organizations. Here, too, after the formal courtesies, we would be told of the activities of the organizations. Thus we heard about land reform, inflation, peace councils, the Federation of Labor. There were no discussions, only lectures and a few limited questions. In the evenings we had the usual banquets and speeches, or occasionally an opera or concert or motion picture given in the hotel or at the state banqueting hall. We had very little time to ourselves, though I was able to escape the routine several times and called on various other foreigners resident in China.

I looked forward to these visits as it was through them that I heard something of what was daily happening in China. I had known the Indian Ambassador and many other Embassy officials. Through them I met Mr. Lamb, the British Chargé d'Affaires, Mr. Rezzonico, the Swiss Minister, Mr. Mahdi, the Indonesian Chargé, and many others. They talked as diplomats but I could still learn much from them about the achievements of New China. When I returned to China for my second visit these acquaintances proved more useful than before. I was on my own and was not so occupied as on the first occasion. The few evenings I spent with them then brought back the reality and restored my objectivity. I constantly dreaded the oppressive atmosphere which sought to imprison man's mind. Free company was the only way to escape the tyranny of repetition. I now know what George Orwell's *1984* would be like.

I recall a strange event in October. It was on the second day of our arrival in Peking that as a member of the non-official Indian good will mission, I was handed a packet containing two million yuans (about ninety dollars). I was completely taken aback. I inquired of more knowing colleagues what it all meant. I was told by them that the People's Democracies expect their friends from capitalist countries to be poor. Hence, this money is given them so that they can buy gifts to take home to their friends. If I did not accept it, it would be considered an insult. I thought the insult was on the other side but before I did anything I consulted an Embassy official. He agreed with me that I should return the money, and I did.

When I returned to China in May, I was free to do as I liked. I had no program. My first week in Peking, while waiting for my credentials, was spent reading; and curio dealers came to me with many treasures, knowing I was interested in them. I whiled away my days with the beauties of Old China.

When the permit came I began to go around with the Indian Delegation to retrace the grounds I had covered before. I do not think I would have been allowed to go alone. But evenings were my own and I met all my old acquaintances in the diplomatic services, who talked to me more freely than before.

M. Rezzonico was a constant delight. He describes himself as being descended from Casanova on one side of his family, and from one of the Popes on the other. He kept a beautiful house and talked well. The Swiss Minister has a hard task, for he looks after the Roman Catholic missions which have gone through much difficulty during the last thirty months. Mr. Lamb, the British Minister, and Mr. Gillette, his aide, with their wives, formed a solitary quartet. They were old China hands and knew a great deal about China's problems though now they were completely cut off from the people. The beautiful grounds of the British Embassy were their little prison.

PEKING

Peking was grim, sullen and silent. But in it live all the men in China who matter. They are seeking to alter the destiny of Asia, and even to catch a fleeting glimpse of them or to hear a few words may throw a revealing light on the unknown sword which hangs over us all. We cannot know them much but we can ignore them only at our peril.

3

MAO TSE-TUNG

DURING our stay in Peking I had read and heard of the new myth into which Mao was growing. He was the Saving Star, the Father, the man of wisdom who led the Communists to success, and many other things. Maoism was fast becoming a new religion and as such unassailable and incontrovertible. Mao had once talked to newspapermen with obvious delight and enjoyed their company. He had freely mixed with the peasants and the workers and known their feelings first hand. He had received hundreds of people in his humble abode in Yenan and answered thousands of letters personally. But today, with Kingdom come, nobody knows whether he lives in the Forbidden City or in a temple in the Western Hills. He no longer mingles with people, nor has he any time to meet or write to the peasants and workers who send him all their problems. He seldom attends any public function except the May Day and October 1st parades and the state receptions on these occasions. Even then, his coming is announced only a few minutes before his appearance. Mao is being built up into a mystery and a new god.

Everywhere one went, in homes and offices, on the streets and railway stations, there was the portrait of Mao with his head uplifted, youthful and smiling. Mao had said, "The people must rule. There is no rule without the people." But now there were no people, only the Leader. He had given his teachings in the *Thoughts of Mao* and his doctrine was a recapitulation of Marx, Engels and Lenin. How could I, a mere mortal, seek to be ushered into his presence and that for the purpose of a requested interview? It was enough that I had seen him twice.

On September 30, 1951, at the state banquet, I stood in front of him a few feet away, drinking a toast to New China while he murmured a few words welcoming the Indian Delegation. Robert Payne had described him as thick and muscular-shouldered with leonine head, blue-black hair, a long sloping forehead, pursed-up lips and large eyes. When I saw him in the midst of a formal banquet surrounded by Chu Teh, Chou En-lai and others, he seemed to me heavier in his loose-fitting, blue serge Sun-Yat-sen suit than in his photographs. He looked like a benign father welcoming his children to the festive occasion with a gentle smile. His rather large eyes saw straight into the visitor's face. He shook hands firmly and warmly with hands which were small and pudgy. Formal toasts over, he lumbered around from table to table returning the earlier toasts and shaking hands all over again. The state banqueting hall was filled with seventeen hundred peasants and labor heroes who were thrilled to the core at beholding their Savior in their midst freely mixing for a passing moment. They had been privileged to come from all over the country to join in the October 1st parade. As Mao went round the hall, the crowd began to sing:

THE GREAT PEACE

*"Tung fang hung t'ai-yang sheng
Chung-kuo Ch'u-lai i-go Mao Tse-tung.*

"The sun is rising red in the East
China has brought forth a Mao Tse-tung.
He labors for the welfare of the people.
Aiyayo! He is the people's great savior.

Mao Tse-tung wan shui! Mao Tse-tung wan shui! May
Mao Tse-tung live ten thousand years!"

I saw him again the next day taking the salute in the
Tien An-Man Square. He stood on the podium surrounded
by the members of his Politburo. There was Chou En-lai
with his bushy eyebrows, handsome and well turned out.
Nearby stood Liu Shao-chi, the Party intellectual, whose
difficult task is to translate Maoism into Stalinism and vice
versa. Mme. Sun was also there to grace one of those rare
occasions when she can be seen by the public in the place
of honor and in the company of other national leaders. The
thin line of the hierarchy was spread out on the rostrum
while Mao stood immobile and watchful. Stalky Chu Teh,
with his weather-beaten face which had seen many battles,
was leading the parade in a jeep. He was followed by
China's armed might.

Mao was again in his blue suit with a peaked cap. Just
below on the podium hung his portrait, enormous, with the
head uplifted toward the rising sun. From 10 A.M. to 3 P.M.
he stood, occasionally lifting his hand in a benedictory
salute which looked almost like the high priest blessing the
worshipers, while thousands of voices shouted, "*Mao Tse-
tung wan shui!*" below in the square. His rustic peasant face
sometimes lit up with a smile that crinkled his eyes into
slits. His presence filled the vast square and gripped the

minds and hearts of the people with a firm determined hand. His word was not only Law but Wisdom and Truth, all rolled into one. To disagree was blasphemy, at least in the eyes of his followers.

Mao is sixty today and a long and arduous life in Yenan has told on his health. His private life with his fourth wife is a mystery. Though he still retains his youthful looks, and a crop of dark black hair makes him look younger than he is, it is said that he cannot stand the strain of standing for hours on end during these parades. The May Day parade was therefore cut down to a mere three hours instead of the usual six.

When the official Indian Delegation presented him with rich presents on behalf of the people of India, Mao hardly looked at them and waved them aside. The members of the Delegation, I believe, were very much concerned for they felt that the presents had not sufficiently attracted him to merit a word of appreciation. Later on, they attended a performance which included an Indian Dance by one of the members of the Delegation. Mao watched from a middle row. One of the Indian delegates, looking at him for his reactions to the performance, reported that his face remained impassive and immobile. I remember a portrait of him in the lounge of the Mukden Hotel. It was a full-length picture of Stalin and Mao walking down the many-pillared corridor of the Kremlin with Molotov and Chou En-lai in the background. Originally there had hung a full-length picture of Stalin, which must have been inherited from the days of Soviet occupation of Manchuria. But when I went back to Mukden in May, 1952, I found it had been removed, and in its place this new picture of Sino-Soviet accord was hung. The artist had taken care to paint

both the Chinese leaders taller than their Soviet counter-
parts. It amused me for I had seen a similar Russian painting
in which the Russians were taller than the Chinese. Each
had to assure his people who was the big brother.

I do not think there had been much love between Stalin
and Mao before the former's death. Soviet Russia had
ignored him throughout China's struggle, for even at the
end of the war it did not expect the Chinese Communists
to complete the conquest of Chiang so soon. Ever since
1927, Mao had found himself in opposition to the Comintern and to Stalin, who had advocated only limited seizure
of lands and armed proletarian uprisings in the cities. After
the departure of Borodin and Roy, this policy was represented by Li Li-san who was a Moscow-trained romantic.
Mao, who had never left his country till he went to Moscow in late '49, drew his strength from his peasant origin.
He knew the hunger of the peasantry for land and realized
that the Communists could continue their resistance only
with the help of the peasant, if he could be rallied to the
cause. "The war of resistance," he wrote much later, "is
really a peasants' war."

Mao analyzed his theory of the Chinese revolution in
1939 in *The Chinese Revolution and the Communist Party
of China:*

Faced with such enemies, questions arise concerning the
special revolutionary bases. The great imperialist powers and
their reactionary allied armies in China have always indefinitely
occupied important Chinese cities. If the revolutionary force
is to accumulate and nurture its own strength and avoid fighting decisive battles with powerful enemies when its own
strength is not yet ascertained, then it must turn the backward
remote areas into progressive, strong bases, making them great

military, political, economic and cultural revolutionary strongholds. Then, from these strongholds, the revolutionary force can start to drive out those malicious enemies who are based upon the cities and who encroach upon the villages. Also, from these strongholds the revolutionary force may, through prolonged struggle, gradually achieve total success. Under such conditions, and because of the unbalanced nature of Chinese economic development (the rural economy is not entirely dependent upon the urban economy), and because of the vastness of China's territory (there are immense spaces for the revolutionary forces to fall back on), and because of the disunity and conflict existing within the anti-revolutionary camp, and because the main force of the Chinese revolution, which is the Chinese peasantry, is under the leadership of the Communist Party, so there arises the great possibility that the Chinese revolution will succeed first and foremost in the countryside. Thus the revolution is driven to its conclusion within a totally unbalanced atmosphere, which increases our difficulties and causes the prolongation of the revolution.

This was a vitally different approach to the whole concept of revolution. The Comintern could have nothing to do with such heresy and the Chinese were left unaided to work out their own destiny. But the Chinese Communists learned the correctness of Mao's analysis through five bitter campaigns launched by Chiang to annihilate them. In the apostolic hierarchy today the doctrine of Chinese communism is handed down from Marx, Engels and Lenin direct to Mao. The Western branch of communism is represented by Russia, while Maoism carries the East. Russia and Mao are allies mutually suspicious of each other, but Mao and Communist China, now completely cut off from the Western powers, are more and more dependent upon Russia for military, technical and economic help. Mao sees in friendship with India a possible counterbalance to the Russian domination. It is this fact perhaps which leads China to seek better relations with India.

I did not see Mao again but I was in Peking when the Indian Cultural Delegation went to see him. Mrs. Pandit, its leader, entered first and after a few minutes the rest of the Delegation was ushered into his presence. Mrs. Pandit had little chance for conversation with him while they drank toasts in champagne to China and India. As he shook hands, someone among the delegates, I am told, murmured that they were happy to be in China. Mao is reported to have replied, "Let us work together for peace. Let us work together for construction." Some people describe this as Mao's "Asian sense." I am not certain what this is supposed to mean, other than that Mao regards Asia as China's sphere of influence.

Mao's attitude to India in recent years shows the changes through which his doctrine is emerging. In the past he had repeatedly asserted that "without the assistance of Soviet Russia, final victory in China is impossible." At the Third Session of the First National Committee of the People's Political Consultative Conference he had again pledged, "In the international fields, we have relied on the firm unity within the camp of peace and democracy headed by the Soviet Union and on the profound good will of the peoples throughout the world." But three years of experience with Soviet Russian alliance had also taught him to fear the domination of Russia over what is now his domain. In October, 1951, therefore, word was sent round that China must cultivate the people of India, and for the first time the list of slogans for the October parade included "Long live the unity of the Asian people." The Indian

visitors to China were fussed over and toasted as representatives of the people of India, though complete silence was
maintained about the government and the Prime Minister
of India. What did this change signify? Mao is today the
Chairman of the Central People's Government and People's
Revolutionary Military Council, and as such wields unlimited power. Success has made him a dictator whose will
is law. Mao had been moved by the desire for power in the
past but then he was a peasant bound to the fortunes of his
Party. Today he is the Saving Star and the untrammeled
power he wields can only be furthered by alliance with
Asian powers and not by obeisance to the Soviet Union.

I was to come across his powerful influence on the life of
the people in far-off places. In Kao Kang, a Northeast Village, women rushed to shake our hands because they heard
that we had shaken hands with Mao. Peasants talked about
letters they had addressed him pouring out their troubles
to him, and the replies they had received. Children from
the day they were able to talk were taught the song, "*Tung
Fang Hung.*" In Shanghai an old woman came to see us
because Mao had told her when she was visiting Peking
during the October parade, "India is the most important of
our neighbors and we must know India better." This was
Chang Mama, the Chairman of the Women's Association
for Resistance, who had been left for dead in a heap of
corpses by the Kuomintang troops.

Mao exercises such powers as no Chinese in the past has
ever had. Is he succumbing to his own myth?

4

CHOU EN-LAI

I am more interested in people and what happens to them than in visiting places. But in China nothing ever happened to the people as far as the visitor was concerned. They were all working to make the new democracy a success. Everything was according to schedule, plans were carried out ahead of time, targets were surpassed and the people's heroes were daily breaking records by contributing hundreds of "inventions." The newspapers contained nothing except reports of the cordial atmosphere in which various receptions were held and the speeches of the ministers delivered at such receptions. The Korean truce negotiations followed the same pattern of monotonous repetition. The world beyond was a closed door to the people living in this city. If I wanted only to see what was pointed out to me I need not have come all the way to China. I could have read the handouts and seen the photographs.

I was here in China hoping to see and listen to living people, not marionettes. I wanted to go backstage, to talk to the people and feel their reactions. Here was Peking,

bristling with men who had changed the course of history—
and I could not ask them a question! I was bored and frustrated. I went up to the chief interpreter to our Delegation
and told her again and again that I wished to interview Mao
Tse-tung, Chou En-lai, Liu Shao-chi and others and I always got the same reply: "Your request has been for-
warded." Ultimately I asked to be taken to the official in
charge of all the visiting delegations. I explained to him
that my request was not unusual. I spoke on behalf of the
Indian newspaper world and assured him that what the
leaders of China have to say would receive the widest publicity in India. It is not enough, I explained, to tell of what
we saw; we must also convey the moving forces behind the
New China in the words of the Chinese leaders. Perhaps
something of my urgency did have effect. He asked me to
put down my questions in writing and offered to send them
to the Foreign Office. He could not say anything more.

For days I heard nothing further about my request for
an interview. Our stay in Peking was nearing the end and I
was frankly disappointed. One day Madame Liu, the chief
interpreter, knowing my irritation at receiving no reply,
called on me and told me that New China does not believe
in press interviews. She hoped, however, that I might still
be able to meet Prime Minister Chou En-lai at a reception.
I said that such meetings in big gatherings have little value
for the press and suggested that if he could not give me an
interview on the basis of my questions, he might call a press
conference where we could all question him. But my request again seemed to vanish into empty air.

Two or three days before our departure, the Indian
Counselor had invited the members of the Goodwill Delegation to an informal dinner at his house. That afternoon we

were suddenly informed that we should be back from the dinner by 9 P.M. as the Foreign Office was holding a reception in honor of all the delegations then in Peking. It was hinted to me that at the reception I would have the opportunity to meet the Prime Minister. I was not much excited about the prospects of the evening, but took the precaution of carrying with me a copy of the questions I had sent.

We drove up to the state reception punctually at 9:30. All the delegations, including Eastern European, Russian, Indonesian, Burmese, Pakistani and Indian were there. We mechanically shook hands and moved on to the sitting room, waiting for the usual speeches which had been repeated at every banquet we had attended. After a few minutes, Madame Liu came in accompanying the Prime Minister and introduced us to him. It was indeed a surprise to us all when we realized that it was the Prime Minister who had received us at the door. This was a change from the imperial protocol we were used to in New Delhi. We were asked to move into the dining hall and take our seats anywhere we liked. As I passed the head table, I saw my original handwritten questions lying on the table before the Prime Minister's chair. I was surprised and worried about how I was to ask all those questions in the midst of two hundred people, many of whom were likely to be little interested in them. But I was determined to snatch every opportunity even if others felt I was depriving them of their chance to put their own queries.

It was a very businesslike session. Chou En-lai got up and addressed the guests. He welcomed us to China and hoped that we had been able to see everything we wanted. Naturally there were many shortcomings, he continued, but New China was only two years old. There might be many things which the visitors would like to know from him and he was prepared, he said, to answer all such questions. It was a short speech which lasted only five minutes. It was translated to us in English and Russian. Immediately after the translations were finished, Chou En-lai waited for a moment as if for questions from us and then turned toward me. He expected me to get up and put my questions.

This was the first time I was seeing Chou at close quarters. Like India's Nehru he is a very handsome man. He was dressed as elegantly as was possible in the Sun Yat-sen uniform. His suit was perfectly tailored and his conscious elegance, coupled with mandarin grace and charm, must impress the simple country people with his unassuming superiority. His well-modulated voice, cultured gestures, boyish, infectious laughter and twinkling eyes, held the on-looker in the spell of his charm. He knows the world and speaks French and German fluently. He was a student in France when together with Li Li-san and Lo Man he founded the Chinese Communist Party. He represented Yenan at Chungking in the difficult days of co-operation with Kuomintang. It is said that Chiang Kai-shek considered Chou the only Communist with whom it was possible to talk.

Chou seems to retain his youthful figure in spite of the arduous life at Yenan and later at Chungking. He shakes hands firmly and moves about the room jauntily. His heavy dark eyebrows reveal the warmth of his affection and his passionate loyalty to the cause. He enjoys speaking and is conscious that he grips the audience with his intellectual and well-thought-out approach to his subject. When I saw him again in 1952 at the opening of the Indian Art Exhibition, I was surprised that he took pains to see as many paintings as possible. He went round the exhibition slowly and commented upon the pictures. His comments showed that he knew little of art and was attracted by the subjects of the pictures rather than the techniques of the artist. I felt that he was consciously making an effort to understand art because he liked to be considered a cultured man.

Chou has very little to do with the Party machine, though he is a member of the Central Committee. He maintains his position by his personal popularity. It is not unusual in the East to find men wielding great influence over the people through their good looks, charm and aristocratic aloofness, quite apart from their integrity and intelligence. In India is Nehru and in Pakistan was Jinnah, both of whom owed their popularity as much to their social position and personal charm as to their intellectual capacity. In the midst of the all-pervading misery and ugliness, such men give hope of some beauty to look up to.

I had sent some sixteen questions which I had worked out step by step so that the answers would not evade any important point. But in the midst of so many people it was impossible to follow them. Apart from some hundred and fifty delegates from various countries, there were present Vice-Premiers Tung Pi-wu and Kuo Mo-jo; Secretary-General of the Central People's Government, Lin Po-chu; and the Vice-Foreign Minister Wang Chia-hsiang. I felt I could not ask at once about the Korean War and the prospects of true negotiations because they might be considered insulting to our hosts. I wanted to wait and see how the meeting developed before considering such questions.

I was on my feet immediately, anxious to seize the opportunity offered, and an interpreter rushed to my side. I began by asking permission to put certain questions to

Chou because, I explained, there was considerable mis-understanding in the world. We in India had heard much about peace while in fact the world was living in a state of conflict. Would the Premier, I asked, explain the Chinese concept of peace? Would he explain how it was possible for conflicting ideologies to co-exist in the world?

I had broken the silence which had descended upon the hall when Chou finished his short address. There were hostile glances from all around for my question implied disbelief in the Communist front of peace conferences and peace pacts. After all, I was in the midst of people soaked in Communist jargon. But Chou En-lai smiled at me. I saw he had followed my English but he waited for the transla-tions into Chinese and Russian to finish. He replied: "You have raised an excellent question. Peace has become a focal problem in the world today. The Chinese people are peace-loving. The principle of the foreign policy of the People's Republic of China is protection of the independence, free-dom, integrity of territory and sovereignty of the country, upholding of lasting international peace and friendly co-operation between people of all countries and opposition to the imperialist policy of aggression and war. Chairman Mao Tse-tung declared to the world on the day when the Central People's Government was established that the government of the People's Republic of China is willing to establish diplomatic relations with any foreign government which agrees to adhere to the principle of equality, mutual benefit and mutual respect for territory and sovereignty. We believe that all countries in the world, whether they are socialist, people's democracies or capitalist, can co-exist peacefully. But the imperialist countries are not willing to have peaceful co-existence and they are afraid of peaceful competition. These imperialist countries are unwilling to discard their aggressive policy of expansion abroad and their war policy. We must then oppose them. We believe that a lasting world peace is in the interest of the peoples of the world and therefore can be achieved, and that the war policy of the imperialists can certainly be defeated. That is to say, if the people of the world fight for peace, a lasting peace will certainly triumph over aggressive wars."

This speech was translated to us by Chou En-lai's secretary, Pu Shou-chang. Pu appears to be a constant companion to Chou for he went with him everywhere when I saw the Premier again in May, 1952. He speaks excellent English and was a student of economics at Harvard. He is one of those who returned to China after the "Liberation" and appears to have accepted communism to serve his country. From what I saw of him, I am sure that he was used to a much better life in the old days but today he has accepted cheerfully the many hardships which life in Communist China involves. Pu, like other young men and women I met, was a constant reminder to me that many of them have found spiritual satisfaction in the prospects of serving their country under the present regime. Pu has many of Chou's characteristics and I could sense the loyalty of the younger one for his superior.

Though I had expected this answer, I had hoped Chou would say something more than the usual jargon of "imperialism and the peace-loving peoples of the Communist world." I wanted to know what was the basic concept of peace and whether such a concept conceded the possibility of the peoples of different persuasions living together. I had hoped that Chou En-lai, with long traditions behind him of the Chinese people who had cultivated the art of living and peaceful coexistence, would say something which would carry with it the ancient wisdom of Confucius and Buddha. But perhaps it was a vain hope. I am myself convinced that peace cannot triumph unless it is conceived in freedom and nonviolence. It will flourish because it recognizes the freedom of another to lead his or her own life. It can exist because it does not seek to assert itself by the force of superior strength but by its determined will to resist all unjust demands. Men must be prepared to sacrifice themselves instead of seeking to impose their will by brute force. I know that Indian freedom, born out of the suffering of thousands of Indians, had led at last to friendship between the British and the Indian. The world sees that the two wars fought in the defense of freedom and peace have not yet led to peace between nations.

Chou's answer left so much unsaid that I had to think quickly of how to frame my next question so as to hold him to the point. Meanwhile the interpreter had moved away to another colleague who wanted to suggest that China should call an Asian Relations Conference to develop friendship among the Asian nations. His question gave me the opportunity to ask whether the unity of Asian peoples could strengthen peace and protect them against aggression. Would not such unity be interpreted as the creation of a regional bloc and as such be considered a threat to peace? When I put this question, I had in mind the new slogan of Asian unity announced on the October 1st parade and what such unity implied in the Communist strategy. The Premier replied:

"We believe that if the people of China, India, Burma, Indonesia, Pakistan and all other Asian peoples, including the Japanese people, strengthen their unity and fight for peace, they will surely be able to resist American aggression and aggression from other imperialist countries. We believe that such strengthening of the unity will certainly contribute to the unity of the people of the world and by no means be a hindrance to it. Since we call for unity among Asian peoples for the purposes of safeguarding world peace and opposing aggressive wars, it cannot therefore possibly constitute a threat to world peace. Those who say that unity among the Asian peoples is a threat to peace are precisely the American and other imperialists who are threatening the peace in Asia by building military bases in Asia, rearming Japan and attempting to extend their aggressive war." Unity according to Communist concept is unity against the West, and peace is Communist peace. Even the new nations of Asia are not recognized as free governments and the appeal is made instead to the peoples of these countries. The omission of Indo-China, Thailand and Malaya was significant.

It was now the turn of another colleague, who called himself an "expert economist," to speak. Instead of asking a question, he delivered a speech on the multiclass structure of Chinese society and the multiparty state under the leadership of the working class. He concluded by asking how long it would take to transform the People's Democratic State into a socialist state, and what was the economic program concerning finance, trade, technical personnel and population. Chou denied that Chinese economy was a mixed economy and said: "The future of China's economic development will be state ownership of industry and socialization of agriculture. This, however, will take a very long time and it will be with the consideration and consent of the Chinese people that we enter into socialism properly and with sure steps."

Chou's answer gave me the opportunity to ask whether, in view of the unbalanced economy, China would welcome foreign assistance and technical skill. Chou replied: "In the process of industrializing our country there are difficulties. But we are confident that we will be able to overcome them mainly with our own strength. Of course," he added, "we welcome very much any assistance from friendly countries and from the people of the world who are sympathetic toward our cause. As far as equipment and technical skill are concerned, we have received great assistance from the Soviet Union, East Germany and Eastern Europe. Southeast Asia has also helped us through the exchange of raw materials during the last two years. For example we learned railway administration from the Soviet."

Reverting to the population problem Chou gave the usual Marxist reply. Kuo Mo-jo, writer turned economist for the occasion, had declared in 1949, "The food problem in China is not due to overpopulation but to excessive economic exploitation by foreign capitalism acting in connivance with the bad eggs in China. The Chinese people have now turned the tables on their exploiters and in the near future there will be no food problem in China even though there is an increase in population." Chou said on this occasion, "We have a vast area and much uncultivated land. Our river valley and irrigation projects will need much labor. A population problem therefore does not exist." Cheap labor is the only capital in an underdeveloped country and the Marxian doctrine advanced here was only finding the capital and not seeking the betterment of the standard of living of the people.

I had been waiting for a chance to question Chou about the Korean War and truce negotiations. Time was running out and to refrain from asking the question would deprive the story of this public interview of any concrete value. I toyed with the idea and finally decided to bring the conversation nearer the subject rather than put the question suddenly. So my next question was: Democracy implies the right of the individual to choose his own good. Dictatorship on the other hand implies the right of one individual or a party to choose what is good for the many. How then is it possible to combine the two concepts as is attempted in China under the name of democratic dictatorship? The name is a contradiction in terms.

I knew this question was purely theoretical and I guessed what Chou's answer would be. But it was the opening by which I wished to convey to him that I was not prepared to accept all the talk about democracy in a Communist country. I do not have his exact words duly corrected by him. But my notes are fairly exhaustive and I have tried to reproduce them precisely. Chou replied: "Democracy and dictatorship are two sides of the political power in China. Peasants, workers, petty bourgeoisie and the national bourgeoisie are under the leadership of the Communist Party. These classes have democratic rights. They have all freedoms, freedom of speech, press, assembly and religious belief. They elect their government. This is what is meant by people's democracy. The Chinese people exercise dictatorships over the overthrown classes, i.e., landlords, bureaucratic capitalists and the Kuomintang. Individual members of these classes are, however, given chances to reform. Thus among the people there is democracy; over others, there is dictatorship. The two are not contradictory, but work in unison."

I had no desire to argue that the leadership of the Communist Party implied no freedom of choice. But while Chou was replying I thought over my question on Korea and framed it as mildly as it was possible to do. In my written questionnaire Korea was the subject of almost half the questions but in the midst of so many people, with interruptions always imminent, I could bring the matter up only once. My question was: What does China seek to establish in Korea? Does China consider the return of the UN forces to the 38th parallel a necessary preliminary to peace in Korea? If this is done would China guarantee the maintenance of the 38th parallel as a boundary between the North and South until peaceful unification of the whole of Korea is achieved? Is it not possible to separate the question of settlement of all East Asian problems from the Korean question so as to bring a speedy end to the sufferings of the Korean people?

This was in October, 1951. The armistice negotiations still continue with no end in sight. Chou En-lai's reply could therefore still have some significance had he really answered these questions. But he only repeated the usual charges of U.S. aggression and China's peaceful intentions, and concluded: "The Chinese people hope now that the armistice negotiations in Korea will speedily reach an agreement on a fair and reasonable basis. Cease fire and armistice are the first step toward the peaceful settlement of the Korean question. Only after this first step is accomplished can we proceed further to the peaceful settlement of the Korean question and other problems of the Far East. Of course, the American imperialists are not willing to follow this path. But we are confident through the concerted and unceasing efforts of the Chinese people, the Korean people, other Asian people and the people of the world, we shall open up this path."

It was almost 2 A.M. and I felt I must cease my questioning. Chou turned to others in the room and invited questions from them. The Indonesian delegate, who had been silent up to then, got up with a quiet dignity and spoke for ten minutes in his own language. He was a good speaker and the Indonesian language has strength and power. When the speech was translated everyone present there realized that something had happened. There was a tense silence. The Indonesian had asked: "What is China's policy toward the overseas Chinese living in various countries of Southeast Asia? Will these Chinese accept the nationality of the country in which they live or will they be the means of Chinese imperialist expansion in Asia?"

Imperialism and communism acting jointly are, in fact, what is happening all over Asia and Eastern Europe. The question was harsh and insulting. And Chou reacted with equal violence at first, though he was too good a host to forget himself for long. The momentary flash of anger expressed itself in a beautiful flourish of his hands and a harsh note in his voice which soon died down. But the anger permitted me to have two answers to the question, the one I took down and that which was sent to me when my copy went for official correction. Chou had told us we could of course file reports of the press conference, but before so doing asked that "we send the copy for correction since the talks had suffered in translation." The difference between the two versions throws a light on the Chinese policy. My notes read:

The problem of nationality is of recent origin. Some countries in Southeast Asia have adopted their own nationality laws. We are quite willing to enter into negotiations to consider this problem. We understand that people struggling for liberation are skeptical to outside influence. But we should believe in truth. You have been in China for three weeks and seen the black and white of things. We should have knowledge of what we have seen. We sympathize with Indonesia's struggle against the Netherlands. We sympathize now with their struggle against American imperialism. Indonesians have suffered from Japanese aggression. Chinese too have suffered from similar aggression. We are nations which have been oppressed by foreign imperialism. We should therefore understand each other. You should know the Chinese people. We shall not defend our ancestors who committed aggression against the Korean and the Vietnamese people in the past. We disavow them. We pledge we shall not commit such mistakes. People's China shall never be imperialist. Since we oppose aggression we shall never start aggression against others. Imperialists are spreading rumors against us to facilitate their own aggression and disrupt our unity.

The official version was:

I think that since we are the nations which either had suffered from imperialist oppression, or are still suffering from it, we should be able to understand each other. Mohammed Tabrani of the Indonesian Delegation should therefore be able to realize how deeply sympathetic the Chinese nation is, which has stood up, after having been oppressed for a long time, for the oppressed people in the world and especially for those in Asia. We do not deny that in the feudal times of our history, our ancestors started aggression against our brother countries in Asia, such as Korea and Vietnam. But that was a mistake committed in feudal times, and that was a crime of the feudal rule in China. All this we have already disavowed. We have already driven out the imperialists and overthrown the feudal forces. The new People's China today will absolutely not do such a thing. I believe that those of you who are present this evening, including our friends from Indonesia, have noted here in Peking and will further notice when you are visiting other places how enthusiastic the Chinese people are to welcome you. The New China opposes aggression and will not start aggression against others. Finally let me remind you that the imperialists are spreading rumors to the effect that China will start aggression against others. Their purpose is to create disunity among us. But can you believe them? They hope to instigate conflicts and mutual suspicions among us in order to facilitate their aggression. Let us, the peace-loving people, unite and bear in mind a common saying, "Beware of pickpockets."

I sent my press copy for correction the next day and received it back three days later, heavily marked in red pencil, together with the approved version of the discussion. I was told to use what I liked from the official statement. In the interim, while I was waiting for the return of my notes, I was anxious lest others use the story before I could. Pablo Neruda and Ilya Ehrenburg had both been present as special guests, and Ehrenburg had sat in a place of honor next to the Premier. The other journalists present were for the most part Communists.

Most of the changes in my copy were of words. The Premier had had my questions with him for days and on his table I had seen some papers which must have been his prepared answers. Many of my questions remained unasked and some he omitted answering, such as whether China was prepared to guarantee the maintenance of the 38th parallel. But the question by the Indonesian delegate was sudden and direct. It involved wide issues, for throughout the Southeast Asian countries, these overseas Chinese are playing a vital role which threatens the freedom and existence of many of them. In a moment of anger Chou had sought to deny the challenge and affirm the Chinese willingness to settle the question peacefully. But mature consideration made it clear that it involved a commitment which China had no intention of carrying out. He had also taunted the Indonesian by telling him that Indonesia was still not free and needed to be liberated from American imperialism and that he had not understood what he had seen in China. The disavowal of aggression was too passionate and final. All this had to be tempered in the official version.

Five hours of discussion had produced something. I had felt Chou's easy grace and charm, and realized the control he has over himself. I have seen these momentary flashes of anger in Nehru often, but Nehru loses his control for a time and then smiles an apology for his temper. Chou's anger on the other hand flowed back imperceptibly into his friendly warmth. He made the listener feel sorry for having been the cause of irritation.

I saw Chou many times afterward at receptions and banquets but never had another opportunity to question him. On my second trip I sent him through the liaison office a few questions based on the statement he had made to the Indonesian's question. After a few days I was informed that he would either give me an interview or send a written reply before I left China, but neither ever materialized.

I watched Chou at the opening of the Indian Art Exhibition later and followed him as he went round the exhibits slowly commenting upon the pictures. He asked many questions and commented upon the resemblance of the Indian scene to China. At the end, he entered his comments in the register and confessed that Kuo Mo-jo who was standing beside him could do it better. This was the only time I saw any of the Chinese leaders forget their Communist earnestness and laugh at a joke.

5

CHI PEI-SHE

My first visit to Peking stands out in my memory because of the long evening at Premier Chou En-lai's reception. The second was marked by a morning spent in the studio of Chi Pei-she, the aged painter who had been world-renowned for a score of years before the "liberation" but had fallen from favor with the revolution, only to be restored to it by Ilya Ehrenburg's recent recommendation. The interview with Chou had to be arranged weeks ahead. I went to see Chi Pei-she unexpectedly, in company with a friend, a French Sinologist, and his wife. While waiting for my permits after my arrival, I had amused myself by looking at art treasures of China which the curio dealers brought to my room. Among them were many of Chi's paintings. One evening, I was casually mentioning how much I had enjoyed these paintings when my French friend told me that he was going to his studio in a day or two. I begged him to take me with him, so, early one morning, I set out on a long ride in a pedicab to southwest Peking, far away from the formerly fashionable section, accompanied by the French couple on their bicycles.

THE GREAT PEACE

It was a beautiful spring morning and the fresh air along the broad avenue passing through the Tien An Man Gate was pungent with the smell of jacaranda in blossom. The breath of old Peking was enveloping me in its graceful warmth. After crossing a maze of narrow hutungs, we arrived at Chi Pei-she's house. It looked small and tumbled down from the outside, but it is impossible to tell much about a house from its exterior. A eunuch opened the door to us and his effeminate voice sounded strange in New China. But as the door closed behind me, I realized that this was the real China and all the screaming posters and loud slogans could not make it otherwise. Here were poverty, want and hunger.

Passing through a small courtyard we were ushered into what appeared to be a living room, studio and perhaps everything else combined. I then knew why no visitor would have been allowed to come here officially. Communism only shows one side of the face, lest ugliness on the other side shock the believer. Both under communism and capitalism, beauty was being created out of human distress. Here in this shabby studio, some of the best paintings of modern China were lying rolled up with the dust of years upon them. Four broken chairs and a teapot adorned one corner of the room while the other side contained a long high table covered with green flannel. This was the master's easel.

The master, dressed in a faded brown Chinese robe, was sitting in an old deck chair, and we sat round him. He is ninety-two years old but age has not withered his creative genius. He sat immobile with his long Confucius-like face and gray eyes that looked far into the distance. His white scraggy beard seemed the only living thing about him. His long bony transparent hands rested on the two arms of the chair. It was difficult to speak to him and arouse him. He only spoke the Hunanese dialect and knew no Mandarin. My French friend had brought along another Chinese, an art teacher, who was a member of the imperial Manchu family but knew no English, and I therefore had to have two interpreters which made conversation more than difficult.

I had first seen Chi Pei-she at a state banquet on my previous visit. In his long black silk robe and high velvet cap, he came slowly up the steps leaning on the arms of his trusted housekeeper whom he wanted to marry even at this age. In his other hand, he carried a long red lacquered staff. In the midst of blue-uniformed men and women he looked out of place. He seemed then to walk out of the ancient Confucian lore, a sage to lead the people back to filial piety and ancestral worship. Today he looked as if the battle for men's souls had been lost and he wanted nothing more than to rest.

Chi Pei-she is New China's greatest artist. Yet he belongs to the traditional Chinese school of painting, which is no longer considered art. Communism does not believe in art for art's sake. Chi only paints flowers, birds, shrimps and lobsters and no political posters. Though Ehrenburg rediscovered him after the great painter had gone into oblivion with the revolution, the recognition had brought him honor but not freedom from privation. No one wants his delicate pictures so the old man continues to paint scroll after scroll, only to roll them up and put them away. The People's Democracy has published an expensive volume of reprints for presentation to the honored guests of the people, while the originals can be had for a trifle in Peking art shops.

I wanted to ask Chi to paint a picture for me because I hoped to see him working. It was difficult to ask, however, because the need for double translations made informal conversation laborious, but while we waited quietly, the old man's companion poured out the customary tea for us. I was surprised to see that our cups contained only hot water while there was tea in the master's cup. I realized that he could not afford the luxury of tea leaves for his guests. I therefore made my request at once. As soon as Chi Pei-she heard that I wanted him to paint, he became energetic, lively and anxious to work. The change was sudden and complete.

He rolled up his sleeves and said, "Yes, I will paint for you but it will cost you forty-four thousand yuans per square foot." This was around two dollars and I readily agreed.

"What shall it be? Flowers, birds, lobsters?"

"Paint what you like, what the moment drives you to," I answered. I told him that I was anxious to write about him so that the people in my country would know something of his art. The Indian Cultural Delegation was in China on a good will mission; perhaps he would do something to symbolize the ancient friendship and the interflow of cultures between the two countries. But all my words had little meaning for the old man and he repeated his question again. I did not want to suggest specifically what he should paint, hoping he would create something of his own will. So I said, "Do a landscape; I have seen too many of your pictures dealing with flowers." The old man stopped for a moment and stared hard at me; then he waved his hand at the interpreter and said, "Tell him it will cost double."

I agreed, amused at the calculating old man but understanding his dire need for money. At art shops I could buy his pictures at forty thousand yuans for a three-foot-square scroll, but now I wanted to see him paint and paint not only for the need of it but for the novelty of being asked to do so of one's own will. The old man's sleeves were pinned up and his woman companion brought out the thin paper from the cupboard. She then began to grind his paint. He stood at the table for several minutes with his white paper drawn taut in front of him, a brush in one hand and the other feeling the texture of the paper. Suddenly he put his finger on one spot and began to paint. He looked up at me and said, "I will paint a simple picture, for what is good is always simple." For forty minutes, he worked, occasionally mixing the black paint with water to get different degrees of blackness.

At last there lay before me on the table a landscape of a meadow with two cows resting in the haze of a spring day. I know that to the Chinese a black and white picture is a more sophisticated form of art, but the absolute simplicity of the picture was, in truth, a little disappointing. Without saying a word Chi Pei-she unpinned his sleeves and went back to his chair. His companion picked up the painting and hung it on the line to dry. In my ignorance I was dumb. I even thought I could have bought a better picture by Chi Pei-she in an art shop at a much cheaper price. But I was determined to find a story in this visit. And so began the conversation which laid bare the soul of a great artist and the age-old spirit of China.

I begged the old man to tell me why he had painted the

two cows, one sitting and one with its back turned gazing away in the distance. "Do the cows," I asked, "signify the two civilizations of India and China? Do they mean anything?"

The old man shook his head and said, "There is no meaning in the picture. I am not a politician. They are just two animals, that is all."

"But why," I said, "two cows and not something else?"

Chi Pei-she replied, "I just felt like painting two cows." Then his face lit up and he said, "The cows remind me of my childhood. Don't you know I was a cowherd till I was twelve years old? I have seldom drawn cows in my pictures but today I remembered my childhood."

"Was your childhood a happy one?"

"I was born in a very poor peasant family. A poor peasant does not think of happiness."

"Where did you learn to paint? Why did you want to paint?"

"When I was twelve years old, an incident happened in my life which changed the future. One evening when I returned with the cows, my grandfather found that I had brought home one cow less. I didn't know the cow had wandered away. My grandfather beat me and ill-treated me that evening and so I ran away from home. I became an apprentice to a carpenter's family in the next village."

I knew then what the cows in the picture meant. It was the cow that was running away from him. It was the cow that had brought him unhappiness. It was the beginning of his creative art. I could feel the deep sadness of his poverty-stricken childhood. He had painted for me a picture which took him back to his village after eighty years of life all over the rest of China. He had found little happiness except in the village landscape where he had wandered as a child, caring neither for happiness nor sorrow. I was more than grateful for the picture he had painted for me.

"How did you come to Peking?" I asked again. "Have you not found success and happiness here?"

"I came to Peking at the age of fifty. For more than thirty years I wandered from village to village learning wood engraving, calligraphy and painting. I left my village and found beauty of nature in the Hunanese countryside. I had three masters who taught me to paint. My masters did not belong to the aristocratic and traditional school."

I asked him again why he came to Peking. "I was ambitious," he replied, "as I wanted to achieve something for myself, and in Peking I was successful in selling my pictures. I knew that the mandarins wanted decorative art so I painted pictures which would sell."

His grandson, who had joined us by this time, intervened and said, "My grandfather is not a bourgeois. When he said he wanted to achieve something for himself, he meant he wanted to serve the people."

I saw the young man was wearing a Party badge. He was also an artist but painted pictures of the type which modern China wants. I presumed he painted portraits of Mao Tse-tung. He saw my skeptical smile and told me a story I repeat for what it is worth. "My grandfather," he said, "even in the days of the Manchu period wanted to remain with the people and of the people. The Emperor offered to make him a mandarin, as his pictures were appreciated by the court. My grandfather declined to accept the honor and threatened to go back to the village and lead the peaceful life to which he was accustomed. My grandfather is and has always been of the people."

I do not know if paintings of flowers and birds and shrimps and lobsters have any meaning for "the people." I have not seen Chi Pei-she's pictures hanging in the exhibitions and art galleries of New China. I saw only one huge painting of red and white dahlias in the sitting room of Kuo Mo-jo, the poet politician. The great Chinese artist had not enough money to serve tea to his guests. He had only the honor which came to him because a Russian journalist liked his pictures.

There was no further prospect of learning more from Chi Pei-she for the conversation had now been taken over by his grandson. The old man had grown silent and tired. I had the painting and the message which Chi had given, and we left.

6

THE NEW IMPERIALISM

"The Sino-Soviet Alliance was signed to prevent aggression by the Japanese or their allies in launching an attack against us," said Kuo Mo-jo, the Vice-Premier, in answer to my question. "It is different in character from the North Atlantic Treaty Alliance, for the Atlantic Treaty is an alliance for war. NATO is the sword held to kill. We hold the sword to defend." China leans heavily on Soviet Russia to hold the sword and consolidate her power. Ideological interests and economic dependence firmly tie her to the Communist bloc. New China faces tremendous problems of political and economic reconstruction. She needs an efficient administrative machinery to administer a vast country and to secure a Communist dictatorship over the lives of a people used to individualistic ways of life, tolerance and understanding. Her industrial and financial resources were in chaos, and poverty and hunger stalked the land. Foreign exploitation, occupation and ambitious warlords had left the country open to invasion and reoccupation. The Chinese Communists needed time and help to unify the country and improve the life of the people.

63

Unfortunately the confused and bungling policy of the United States left much bitterness and anger. The United States, UNRRA and even the UN became suspect, for to the Chinese mind they sought to re-establish disorder and corruption. There was no other alternative for Mao but to seek the help of the Soviet Union. As late as 1945 the Russians had relied on Chiang to provide a unified and stable China. Mao had followed his own "star" and led an agrarian revolution as a prelude to the war of liberation. For twenty-three years he had suffered in the wilderness and carried on his own war of resistance, denied any assistance by the Russians. The Comintern had called him an "opportunist" and left him to build his "romantic Soviet republics in the mountainous wilderness" instead of leading a proletarian mass movement. And he had fought not merely many battles but had given the Chinese Communists their own theory of revolution. Now, Mao needed the Russian aid.

In July, 1949, he wrote: "Externally we must unite in a common struggle with the peoples of all countries and with those nations which treat us as equals. This means allying ourselves with the Soviet Union, with every New Democratic country and with the proletariat and the broad masses in all other countries. This means forming an international united front." What had happened to change his views? The American attempts to unify China and bring about a coalition government had failed mainly because the United States continued military assistance to Chiang's forces. This aid had been utilized by Chiang to annihilate the Communists. In July, 1949, the task of unifying the country was still unfinished, since the Kuomintang forces held out in the South. In November, 1948, Mao had declared: "The particular task of the Communists is to unite all revolutionary forces within the whole country, to drive out American imperialism, overthrow the reactionary rule of the Kuomintang and establish a unified democratic people's republic in alliance with the Soviet Union."

It was a total change-over. The task having been achieved, Mao turned to Soviet Russia for help. He knew that he was beset with overwhelming problems which he could not tackle unless he could assure internal security and face with equanimity any attempts of Chiang to return. In December, 1949, he went to Moscow for the first time and after weeks of bitter wrangling brought back the Sino-Soviet Treaty of friendship, alliance and mutual assistance. Economic aid, under a separate agreement, gave a mere 300-million-dollar loan spread over five years. The announcement of the treaty had an immediate political and economic effect within the country, since it made invasion possible only at the risk of a world war.

The alliance is between two unequal partners. Though China has resources and vast manpower, she is today completely dependent upon Russian military and technical aid. Mao knows it, but as a realist he also knows his limitations. He needs military equipment to keep his army a modern fighting machine. In the October 1st parade, picked regiments of the Chinese army and air force marched with much American equipment captured from the Kuomintang. But such equipment easily goes out of date and China must continue to obtain the latest. Russia, too, is interested in maintaining a strong army to guard the eastern frontiers and engage the enemy on a double front over her vast geopolitical mass. So we find today a well-trained, Russian-equipped air force in China.

China needed industrialization to relieve the pressure on land. Her existing industries had to be started anew and heavy industries established. Soviet Russia could spare little in capital goods or technical assistance, though Russian influence is noticeable all over the country. In the North, in Manchuria, Mao's portrait has been inevitably flanked by Stalin's as a constant reminder. Signboards on the railway stations, hotels and theaters are invariably in both languages. In the South, however, the influence is less marked. The portraits here range from Marx to Stalin and Mao to remind viewers of the long road of the Communist faith.

In the colleges and schools Russian has replaced English and the bookshops were filled with Russian books, magazines and pamphlets, with English books virtually unobtainable. Liu Shao-chi, the Party dialectician, is busy explaining Maoism in terms of Stalinism and vice versa, and the history of the revolution is perverted to show the valuable advice and aid given to China by Russia. In the process there is much talk of the leadership of the proletariat and the need to further it.

Mao is conscious of the growing dependence on and the increasing influence of the Soviet power. He has no alternative, however, since the Western powers have thrown him into the arms of the Russian Bear. Around him he sees Liu Shao-chi, Peng Chen and Kao Kang who are strongly inclined toward the left and insist on the Sovietization of China. Among the cadres, schools and colleges a new generation is rising which is trained in Russian methods and under Russian influence. In any conflict for power within the country the Russian influence and good will will have a decisive voice. But as long as the Mao–Chu Teh combination lasts, nothing can happen against Mao's will.

THE NEW IMPERIALISM

Speaking to the Indian Ambassador, Mao, it is reported, recalled his visit to an airplane plant while in Moscow. "Not until your country and mine can do this ourselves," he remarked, "can we act decisively. Until then we must move slowly." So he moves slowly but certainly. He will, however, never be a Tito for history and ideological identity hold him to an understanding with Soviet Russia. Yet he is moving as well toward seeking an understanding with the Asian countries, especially India. In this he is strengthened by the traditional hatred of the Chinese for the foreigner. The Russians were once, also, "foreign devils" often called the "big noses" by the common man in China.

On October 1, 1951, for the first time, Mao gave the slogan of Asian unity. At the celebrations which followed, India was given precedence over all other missions except the Soviet delegation. Welcoming the new Indian Ambassador in September, 1952, Mao repeated, "I am convinced that the friendly co-operation between the peoples of our two countries will be promoted and consolidated more and more in the common cause of striving for peace in Asia and in the whole world." Mao's words were echoed by the people, who showered warmth and affection on us during both my visits. It was a warning and a hint to Soviet Russia that China effectively carries the support of millions of Asia who also had suffered at the hands of the Western powers. The last two years have clearly shown that the Chinese communism has succeeded in Asia where the Russians had failed.

When I met Kuo Mo-jo, I hoped he would say something about the purpose of Mao's "Asian sense." I am convinced that the talk of Asian unity and Asian peace is an attempt to achieve a regional collective security against both East and West. It is Mao's way to enforce equality with the Soviet and peace on the West. Kuo Mo-jo replied: "We seek Asian unity to promote the betterment of the backward peoples and the right of independence and self-determination of the Asian countries. We are not calling for a new Monroe Doctrine for Asia. We are seeking only the right of self-determination for the Asian peoples. We do not want Asia for ourselves. We do not reject Western culture. Thus Asian unity is a step toward world unity."

I pressed Kuo Mo-jo to explain in what way Asian unity could lead to world unity and peace unless the Asian powers seek to be a "third force" holding the balance between the East and the West. Would not a genuine United Nations be a better guarantee of peace? "Asian unity will safeguard peace," he replied. "There are only two forces in the world, forces of peace and forces of war. There is no 'third force.' Asian unity will increase the forces of peace. Not all the Western powers are imperialists. The majority of people in the West also love peace. We therefore lean on the side of peace. The conflict is getting sharper and the only hope of peace is to strengthen the side of peace. There is no middle way. Asian unity is therefore a step in the direction of world peace and world unity."

I recalled what Mao had said in 1949. He had then written:

Forty years' experience of Sun Yat-sen and twenty-eight years' experience of the Chinese Communist Party have convinced us that in order to attain victory and consolidate it, we must incline to one side. According to these experiences, the Chinese people must incline either toward the side of imperialism or toward the side of socialism. There can be no exception to this rule. It is impossible to sit on the fence; there is no third road. Neutrality is merely a camouflage; a third road does not exist.

Mao the realist had been too dogmatic then. The world was either black or white, there were no half tones. But Mao himself had described dogmas as "more useless than cow dung, for cow dung can be used as a fertilizer." Now he was changing. He was talking of Asian unity with nations whom he had once called "running dogs of imperialism." The Soviet alliance had taught him too soon, it appears, where he stood and he was beginning to shed his dogmatism.

Perhaps it was the Korean War which was giving him a new outlook on foreign relations. It is true that Korea and Indo-China have been historically considered by the Chinese as their spheres of influence. Korea was the traditional door to the conquest of China. Indo-China is part of the Chinese rice bowl and has supplied rice to south China. China wants friendly powers in these countries. Yet war-weary China would have hesitated to enter upon a venture which must effect her already exhausted economy, unless she had been given hopes of an early successful termination with promises of military and economic aid. I saw ample evidence of exhaustion and bitter frustration because promises had not come up to expectation.

In the beginning, the war helped in the reorganization of the army and its training in modern warfare. Under the stress of war, industry was reorganized and the initiative of the people released. China was able to impose heavy sacrifices on them in the name of national defense, and the people submitted to compulsory contributions, liquidation of all who disagreed with the government and austerity living. They accepted high prices and hard work, and "the evil of war was turned into good"; but there is a limit to such endurance.

There are now murmurs of criticism and eagerness to return to peacetime reconstruction. I had repeatedly asked why the South Koreans should have invaded the North since, according to the Chinese, the people were not behind Syngman Rhee. Ultimately one of the high-up Communists said, "The North Koreans could have easily dealt with the hirelings of Rhee without going into a large-scale war, but they were impatient." The Panmunjon negotiations were reported in the press with increasing bitterness. The charges of bacteriological warfare were necessary, I felt, to revive the drooping spirits of the people. They are the customary atrocity stories used to rouse the people to yet greater sacrifices.

China's anxiety to end the war in Korea is genuine, but she cannot afford to lose face with her people. The people suffered too long in the name of national honor and unity. The stalemate in Korea has been described to them as victory in which the Chinese people have matched their blood with steel. An old story of the hunter and the tiger was repeatedly told. The hunter (the United States) has placed his hand in the mouth of the tiger (China) and now the tiger can let go the hand only at its own risk. But unfortunately the tiger cannot swallow the hunter. So the cry for Asian unity is not only a plea to readjust the balance between the parties to the Sino-Soviet alliance, but also a cry for help to save China's face in Korea.

The Communist Mao now talks of coexistence with capitalists and their "running dogs." Chou repeated it to me: "We believe that all countries in the world, whether they are socialist, people's democracies or capitalist, can co-exist peacefully." But peaceful coexistence according to Communist China is only possible when Asian unity has strengthened the hands of Mao and compelled the submission of the world to the Sino-Soviet supremacy.

Toward this end China hopes to use the ten million Chinese residents all over Southeast Asia. These Chinese must remain the nationals of China for they will not be allowed to accept any other nationality. Chou En-lai had slipped when he said that China was prepared to negotiate the question of nationality with other Asian countries, but the slip was corrected later. I am convinced that the Chinese residents of Indonesia, Indo-China, Thailand, Malaya, Burma and India will never be given up, though these Chinese have lived for generations in the lands of their adoption. Early in 1952 a group of Indonesian Chinese students arrived in China with the passports of their country. China confiscated these passports and insisted that they carry Chinese passports. The Indonesian Chargé d'Affaires made many protests but to no avail.

On another occasion the Indian Ambassador asked Premier Chou to release the seventy foreigners now in prison on humanitarian grounds. Chou is reported to have replied, "Do not press me for the release of these criminals as long as there are fourteen thousand Chinese in prison in Malaya." In the People's Political Consultative Council, the overseas Chinese have sixteen members. It is thus made clear that China has no intention of giving up her claim to the allegiance of the Chinese who have lived outside China for generations. In Calcutta, where about ten thousand Chinese live, all the techniques of Communist infiltration, indoctrination coupled with compulsion under pressure of threats of dire consequences, are being used to reduce them to submission. A Chinese schoolteacher was driven to suicide because his wife and mother-in-law faced him with serious threats.

China seeks to utilize these overseas nationals to "liberate" the Southeast Asia from foreign imperialism and build Asian unity. The frustrated nationalism and the economic poverty of the people become useful instruments to further these designs. In Indo-China Ho Chi Minh carries on a bitter struggle with the help of the Chinese, though China will not openly intervene. In Thailand, the corruption of the politicians and the opposite pulls of the British and American diplomacy have left the country an easy prey. Meanwhile, Pridi, the only popular Thai leader, bides his time in Shanghai. So it will continue, unless the Asian nations realize that a new imperialism rather than a liberator is seeking to fasten upon them.

Chinese relations with India are a key factor in any developments in Southeast Asia, for in all these countries India, with the important economic interests and political influence of her overseas Indians, is the only counterbalancing factor. In significant contrast to the Chinese, the Indian residents have been advised to accept the nationality of the country of their adoption. China, while outwardly paying tribute to a "two-thousand-year-old friendship" and "the interflow of culture," has little consideration for the government of India or Indian interests.

India, according to the Chinese Communists, is not an independent country. The controlled Chinese press writes disparagingly about Indian elections and Nehru. "Despite 'independence' and 'free elections,'" wrote one paper, "the British and more and more the Americans have been extending their control over the Indian economy." India was labeled the "running dog of imperialism" when she supported the UN resolution calling North Korea the aggressor. Mrs. Pandit, I understand, was repeatedly asked by such men as Kao Kang, Chen Yi, the Mayor of Shanghai, and others about the British interference in India and the influence of Commonwealth ties on Indian foreign policy. These were open hints that India was still to be liberated.

I found a marked difference between the treatment accorded the two delegations I accompanied. One was a people's delegation. It was met with the same red carpet, but with, as well, more popular welcomes and more warmth. The Indian government's delegation was met with cold formality. There were no popular rallies to welcome it. The information given it was limited and it was more "conducted" than the previous delegation.

In Tibet, China and India came into conflict for the first time. Tibet, though racially one with the Chinese, has been politically independent, though it has always been within the Chinese sphere of influence and a Chinese "protectorate." But the ties with China were loose, and China was too weak to exercise any dominating influence. It was only at the beginning of the twentieth century that both Russia and the British in India sought to interfere in the affairs of the country. Tibet is by religion, by language and by culture more Indian than Chinese. It was to Indian interest that Tibet maintained her internal independence and conceded to China only the rights of suzerainty. But recently, after assuring the Indian Ambassador that China had only peaceful intentions in Tibet, China forcibly occupied the country. Today India and her neighbors Nepal and Bhutan face the consequences in the Communist infiltration of their affairs.

Along the two-thousand-mile-long frontier between China and India stands a powerful army, not perhaps to attack, because aggression is not possible, but certainly to influence and promote the "liberation" of India. Mao needs India not only to strengthen his hands politically but also as an economic ally to supplement the meager assistance he receives from his alliance with Russia. Official China is therefore friendly to India while at the same time she offers every assistance to the Indian people's "liberation."

So, while Mao develops his Asian sense, Russia stands firm on Chinese soil, rationing her aid, friendly but unobtrusive, courteous but firm. She needs China's vast manpower and resources for the coming struggle, and she is content to wait. Meanwhile she will do nothing to irritate China, for she realizes that to the millions of common people there Russia remains a Western power and, as such, a "foreign devil" inheriting the traditions of colonialism and exploitation. The Russian Embassy in Peking avoids anything that might be construed as open interference in the internal affairs of China. In such a contingency, Russia finds others to do her work.

The Indian Ambassador in Peking claimed "it is wrong to think the Russians have any influence or power in China." In support of this claim he told a story about the arrest of a Soviet citizen somewhere in inner China. "The Soviet Embassy made inquiries at the Chinese Foreign Office about the arrest of its citizen, but could get no information. Ultimately, the Embassy asked me to intervene personally. I did so, and after repeated representations, succeeded in obtaining the release of the Soviet citizen."

The correct appearances so carefully maintained by the Russians in China is shown by the reaction of our interpreter. A colleague once said to Chang, "You regard India as semicolonial. You think we are still under the British influence. Well, we think you are greatly under the influence of Russia."

Chang reacted violently, "Yes, we are dependent on Russia for technical aid and advice. We have not concealed the fact. But have you ever seen a Russian order about a Chinese?"

No, I had not seen a Russian ordering a Chinese about. He does not need to. He finds other people to do his dirty work.

Part Two

PRODUCE OR PERISH

1

LAND REFORM

LAND reform is the single fact which has transformed the face of old China and rekindled the vitality of a people which had been choked under feudal despotism. Chiang Kai-shek had recognized that "the center of gravity of China's ultimate victory does not lie in Nanking or any other large city. It lies in the stout hearts of the people all over the country." But Chiang rested his power on the feudal landlords and city compradors. He was never able to win the faith of the large masses of peasantry which form the real China. Mao Tse-tung on the other hand has relied entirely on the peasantry. "The war of resistance," he wrote, "is really a peasants' war. Everything we use in resistance, everything we live on is really given to us by the peasants." And again: "The villages and the countryside will defeat the cities and the towns."

In his book, *The Chinese Revolution and the Communist*, Mao analyzed the correct nature of the Chinese society.

Since our present Chinese society is colonial, semicolonial and semifeudal, the chief enemies of the Chinese revolution are

79

still the imperialists and the semifeudal forces. . . . Therefore the nature of the Chinese revolution at its present stage is not that of a proletarian socialism, but of bourgeois democracy. . . . Politically it is formed by several revolutionary classes which unite together to form a revolutionary democratic dictatorship over the imperialists, traitors and reactionaries, and to oppose the transformation of Chinese society into a society of bourgeois dictatorship. Economically, it strives to nationalize all large capital interests, and all the large enterprises of the imperialists, traitors and reactionaries, to divide up the large estates and to distribute them among the peasantry, at the same time helping the middle and small private industries while making no attempt to abolish the economy of the rich farmers.

This was heterodoxy indeed. For a Marxist to rely on the peasantry as the spearhead of the revolution was something novel. But Mao is no dogmatist. He saw that the proletariat in China was limited in number and confined to the cities where they came under the guns of foreign powers. The essence of the struggle for power between Chiang and Mao was to win the faith of the peasantry. And Mao won, because he succeeded in entrenching the Communist Party in the hearts of the farmers with his land reform.

The poverty of the Chinese peasant can scarcely be imagined. In an agricultural population of about 410 millions, only 10 per cent of the population owned 60 to 70 per cent of the land. Of the remainder about 60 per cent were poor peasants or landless laborers. They had very little land and worked as slave labor or leased a small plot of land at extraordinarily high rents to eke out a pitiful existence. It is estimated that on the average they paid 50 to 70 per cent of the yield as rent to the landlord. At times these exactions went as high as almost the whole yield. The peasant lived on a starvation level, an easy prey to epidemics and famines. He was therefore a ready recruit for arson, banditry or an ambitious warlord. It is easy to see why land reform through the distribution of the land among the landless peasantry would release the mighty passion of a people subsisting between life and death.

Mao has kept his promise to the peasant. Today land reform has been carried out in an area inhabited by about 310 million people, and will soon be completed.

"The essential content of the land reform," states Liu Shao-chi in his report to the National Committee of the Chinese People's Consultative Conference in June, 1950, "is the confiscation of the land of the landlord class for distribution to the landless or land-poor peasants. Thus the landlords as a class in society are abolished and the land ownership system of feudal exploitation is transformed into a system of peasant land ownership."

The Agrarian Law claims that land reform is introduced "in order to set free the rural productive forces, develop agricultural production and thus pave the way for New China's industrialization." Since production was the chief aim, the Agrarian Law did not touch the rich and the middle peasant. Mao had declared, "We must no longer requisition surplus land and the property of the rich peasant; we must preserve our rich peasant economy for nothing matters so much as the restoration of production in rural areas." The rich peasant is defined as one who owns land or partially owns and rents some land on which he works himself and also hires labor. The middle peasant may own some land or rent it; he depends wholly or mainly upon his own labor for livelihood. Generally speaking, both the rich and the middle peasants' lands were not requisitioned.

Basically China abolished landlordism, by confiscation of land and other means of production owned by the land-lords, shrines, temples, churches and the rural land belong-ing to industrialists and merchants, and distributed this land among poor peasants who had little or no land and who have no other means of production. The limitations of the Chinese economy have led the Communists to accept the capitalist class and the rich peasant as friendly categories. Both are a necessity for the maintenance of production in the country. But neither of them will have a place in the future when the New Democracy is replaced by the pro-letariat dictatorship.

About half the 240 million acres of cultivated land in China came under the redistribution program. Since the distribution is on a per capita basis, each peasant's share de-pended upon the size of his family and the part of the country in which he lived. The average holding thus differs widely from district to district and between the north and the south. In the northeast near Mukden it was 2.7 mows per head, in the north around Peking 1.9 mows, and in the south it came down to 1.3 mows. (Six mows equals one acre.) Such small farms may satisfy the land hunger but they can hardly be economically sound holdings, which will lead to increased production and full employment.

Due to the poverty of the farmer, agriculture in China had been for a long time based on intensive cultivation on a gardening scale. The land reform by itself was hardly likely to lead to any substantial increase in production, and is therefore not designed to relieve the poor except by the removal of the high rents and other exactions of the land-

mix in to
am

[3]

Land Reform
(Distribution satisfying
but plots very
inefficient.
Could this inefficiency
Land had any effect
in producing the
Chinese communes?

lords. In place of these charges the peasant is today called upon to pay 18 per cent of the produce in kind as land tax to the government. (I might say that no definite figure of the rate of this tax is available. In Peking and other places I have heard it to be only 13 per cent while in *China Monthly Review*, a magazine run by two Americans which wholeheartedly follows the Communist line, it is stated to be 27 per cent.) Whatever the exact amount of tax, the peasant in the village looks more cheerful, better fed and clothed. It must therefore be accepted that he retains a greater share of the produce than formerly.

The Communists admit that the problem of poverty can be finally solved "only if agricultural production can be greatly developed, if the industrialization of New China can be realized, if the living standards of the people throughout the country can be raised and if China finally embarks on the road to socialism." Agricultural production can be increased only by the use of fertilizers and mechanical farming, but the agricultural laborer now turned peasant farmer has neither the means nor the equipment to go in for such cultivation. In addition the small holdings would have to be turned into large farms through co-operatives or collectivization before such intensive cultivation could be made possible. Is this process possible in a country where the peasant is so deeply attached to the land?

The present political consequences of land reform are far-reaching in their effect on the Chinese society. The technique adapted to carry it out brought the peasant, hitherto apathetic, into open revolt against his rulers in the village. Through "Accusation," "Speak Bitterness" and "Struggle" meetings, led by the trained cadres of the Land

Reform Teams, the peasants poured out their ancient pent-up feelings against their landlords. They denounced them and defied the gods and religion which had made them believe in the inevitability of their fate. Much blood was spilled in the process. The few landlords who escaped the wrath, on the grounds that they had not been guilty of heinous crimes, were given a share of the land similar to that of the landless laborer so that they too might reform themselves "through labor." Meanwhile Peasants' Associations were organized and through them the government at Peking was able to centralize the administration of the country far more effectively than ever in the history of China. The peasant, having realized the dream of his life, leans on the Communist Party with trust and is willing to carry out its behests.

Since the purpose of land reform was to develop more productive agriculture and thus pave the way for industrialization and improvement in the standard of living for the millions, claims are continuously made to show an increase in farm production. Agricultural surplus is necessary for adequate capital resources to industrialize the country. Statistics are therefore offered to justify the claims but such statistics have little value in assessing the nation's economic condition because they are always given in terms of the previous percentage and thus make it impossible to estimate the actual quantity produced. In a country where there is no real machinery for the collection of statistics, any attempt to give them can only be guesswork, but in China, of course, these figures have a political purpose behind them. They seek to reassure the people that progress is possible only through the government. As an Indian I was particularly interested in these statistics because through them it is implied that the underfed masses of the Asian countries will find their salvation in following the Communist line.

Peng Chen, the Mayor of Peking, is one of the triumvirate which stands next to Mao and Chu Teh. He is the party puritan and disciplinarian. Clean-shaven, stocky and heavily built, he speaks with stoical determination and complete loyalty to Marxism and Leninism. As Mayor of Peking he holds a vital position in the government of China. He is continuously called upon to handle difficult tasks which require the capacity of command and to enforce organizational discipline. He was in charge of the land reform in the North and in February, 1952, he was again called upon to head the San Fan Wu Fan campaigns purging government and industry.

In a brilliant speech to the foreign delegations visiting China, he claimed China had an exportable food surplus as a result of land reform. For the last seventy-three years, it had been a deficit country. Now, in two years the total agricultural production had gone up by 14 per cent in the first year and 8 per cent in the second. The increase of 22 per cent over 1949 had turned deficit-ridden, food-importing China into a food-exporting country.

I am by nature a skeptic, who rarely becomes too enthusiastic about anything. I have seen and experienced poverty in my own country and wanted to accept these claims, for they seemed to indicate hope for millions of hungry Asians. But then I remembered what Nan Han-chen had said when he had spoken about the control of inflation. Agricultural production in China had gone down by 30 per cent during the inflationary period, and now that the currency was stabilized an increase in production of 22 per cent was nothing extraordinary. Nan Han-chen, as Governor of the People's Bank, ought to know the real facts. According to him, the food grains production in 1951 was 92 per cent of 1936. The figures for 1936 were considered a record production and included Manchurian produce. Yet in 1936, China had had to import food grains. The estimate based on production of individual crops was as follows:

Rice	99.4 in 1951	100 in 1936
Wheat	88.5 in 1951	100 in 1936
Cotton	133.0 in 1951	100 in 1936
Tobacco	130.5 in 1951	100 in 1936
Hemp	227.1 in 1951	100 in 1936

These figures clearly show that the food grains production had not increased sufficiently to provide China with exportable surplus. On the contrary, with the increase in population between 1936 and 1952, the shortage must be much greater than before. One wonders, therefore, how China is able to export food grains. In 1951 she exported to India 500,000 tons of rice and millet. In 1952 the figure was 150,000 tons. These exports have been called political moves made at the expense of the Chinese consumer. News items have been released from Hongkong stating that while there was famine in some areas in China, China was exporting food to India.

Whatever the facts, there do appear to be ample food grains available in the numerous towns that I visited. There was no rationing or any kind of controls. The prices of food grains varied from place to place, but such variations are due to transport limitations and attempts to rely on local economy.

The exportable food grains come from the surplus the

government of China has left from the revenues it receives. The land tax is collected in kind. These receipts are used for the nonagricultural population in urban areas; in 1950, for example, the government was under obligation to supply food grains to about eighty million people. By reduction of the famine area of about twenty million acres in 1949 to seven million acres in 1952, it was able to reduce its obligations further. Austerity living, control of consumption and the ending of public wastage also helped. The residue of food grains left after all obligations are met is exported.

I was convinced from what I saw in the agricultural village I visited that the increase in agricultural production is due primarily to normal conditions of life now prevailing in China. There is peace and order. Bandits and armed men of the warlords no longer ravage the countryside. Secret societies are no longer a menace. The peasant carries on his work without the old fear of murder and rape. He has more things he can call his own, for he retains a greater part of the fruits of his labor. Above all, the land which he works is his own. He is happy because he has a little more cloth to wear, a little more food to eat.

The gods he once worshiped and obeyed now hold no fears for him. He no longer feels that it is his inexorable fate to be poor. What Buddha has denied him for centuries has become his own by his efforts. Old temples and idols have been rejected and their place taken by allegiance to the Communist Party which has brought this new hope to his enervated body. Not much effort beyond the actual deed was needed to achieve this. The concrete facts of land reform impressed him and he removed the idols from the temples and turned them into schools and community centers.

One sees in China today the vast change the new property relations have brought. I went to an old temple in the small coal-mining town of Tatung. It was an ancient building adorned with gilt and color as Buddhist temples in China were. The few priests living in the monastery attended to all the ceremonies. The monks told me that no one now came to worship. They maintained themselves partly by working on the little land left to the temple and partly on the allowance given to them by the government. Most such temples had been turned to other uses but the Tatung temple was allowed to remain because it was a historical relic dating from the eleventh century.

In the Tatung temple we could see the remains of many incense sticks on the incense burner. We were a little surprised that the worship of Buddha was still permitted. We asked the monk if many people came to the temple, and he began to tell, in a timid voice, how few did come to offer their prayers because most people were afraid to. Suddenly he saw our interpreter approaching us. Our conversation up to then had been translated by one among us who knew some Chinese. Now the story of the monk changed. Now there was no one at all to worship, and the incense sticks I had seen were only the remains of his own prayers.

The abolition of landlordism also broke up the old tradition which imposed obedience to the parents and the authority of men over women. Elsewhere other influences have helped to alter family relationships but in the villages the land reform was the vital force which snapped the chains. Women have taken to literacy classes and were as anxious to show off their knowledge as little children. In the crowds which collected around the visitors, they were eager to speak up and tell us all that they had achieved. There is an old saying that "a poor man has no right to talk." But New China was both looking up and talking. This was more important than the claim that production had gone up or that prosperity was around the corner.

Mao had spoken only of "restoration of production in rural areas." But the Agrarian Reform Law had claimed as its purpose the development of agricultural production to pave the way for industrialization. I have tried to show from statistics supplied by the Chinese themselves that there cannot be any surpluses which would promote national savings and thus create the capital necessary for China's industrialization. Land reform is a political and revolutionary force and not an economic change. Even the progress toward co-operative farming has its limitations, particularly in the South where farms are extremely small. The individualism of the peasant and his age-long attachment to land makes the shift to large-scale farming and crop planning slow and difficult.

Chinese leaders recognize the danger of increasingly small holdings but hope that the farmer will realize the advantages of mechanization of agriculture and thus accept the need for collectivization. Nan Han-chen of the People's Bank relies on mechanization to promote capital for industrialization, but today there is no saving toward the accumulation of capital. The export of food grains to India is so small that any conclusion drawn from it about agricultural surplus is unjustified.

Though the land reform has not achieved its economic purpose, it has achieved a social revolution by satisfying the primary urges of the peasant. There may not be enough today to fulfill all his wants and his bowl of rice may be only a little bigger than before, but an age-old dream has nonetheless been realized. The peasants of China therefore have acquired a new faith which is today the bulwark of strength behind Mao's government.

Confucius was once asked to enumerate the three things vital to a ruler. The sage replied, "Sufficiency of food, sufficiency of military power and sufficiency of popular faith in the ruler."

When asked what he would omit if only two were possible, he replied, "Omit military power."

He was asked again what he would omit if only one were possible. Confucius replied, "Let the people lose their food but keep their faith."

The people of China have that faith—at least for the present.

2

VILLAGES ON DISPLAY

I VISITED two villages where land reform had led to different developments in the rural economy, one near Peking and the other near Mukden in the Northeast. As I was taken to both villages on each of my visits, it may be assumed that they were showplaces for the demonstration of the new economy. The first village was only a few miles outside the city and mainly supplied vegetables to the city. We approached the village along a dusty road between the fields. A large cluster of the villagers had turned up to receive us. As we alighted, we were greeted by the hand clappings that are the usual Chinese manner of greeting. They surrounded us and shook hands and their smiles revealed their happiness at seeing us. We should have reciprocated the warmth of their welcome by clapping our hands in turn, but we were shy and awkward and had not yet learned the custom. In the crowd, the men were mostly dressed in blue but the women clung to their old-fashioned dresses of printed cotton. Many children flaunted the red cravats of the "Young Pioneers."

We were not allowed to stay long with the peasants

despite their pleasure at being with us. We were quickly steered toward the Peasants' Association office while the crowd around us melted away as if by previous arrangement. A few children remained peering at us with curiosity, eager to meet and know us a little better. One or two of us left the office, preferring the spring sunshine to the closed atmosphere of the room, and we joined the children hoping to talk to them. They were persuaded to sing and dance for us briefly, but this too was stopped and they quietly edged away.

Chinese children are perhaps the most attractive children in the world. Their rice-fed chubbiness, flat noses and smiling eyes hide the undernourished and often unhealthy conditions of their bodies. These youngsters were eager for affection and understanding but fraternizing with a foreigner was perhaps not a permissible joy. I do not know what terror frightened them into sudden withdrawal. They left us to our interpreters and their report of the joy and happiness of New China. It was always difficult to cross the invisible barrier between us and the people.

The population of this village was 2,050, and the 430 families had between them 2,190 mows, or 365 acres, of land. The average per capita holding was about 1.7 mows. Before the land reform there had been 20 landlord families who among themselves had owned 1,435 mows of land. Today some of them had the same small holdings as the peasants while others had paid the penalty for long oppression of their fellow men. The Peking government had given 126 million yuans as a loan to the village. One million yuans is about $45 or £16.

The village had undergone land reform early in 1950 and in many peasant homes I visited I saw signs of what it meant. They had timepieces and old porcelain ware which must have come to them as their share from the dispossessed landlords. One of the families even had a small crystal radio set with earphones.

The district officials claimed that since the land reform, production had increased because the peasants now worked harder and new irrigation facilities had been made available. The village had purchased many draught animals and carts, and new wells had been dug. Liberation had brought a primary school of four classes in which 160 children were being educated while 420 adults also attended literacy classes. There had been a Patriotic Drive and the peasants had contributed 54.5 million yuans to the Aid Korea and Resist America Fund. A peasant family was now earning as much as twenty million yuans a year.

It was difficult to believe the above figure of family earnings. The Chinese often read 100,000 as one million and an income of twenty million yuans may well be two million. This figure appears to be more probable because the standard of living of the peasantry in this village was inferior to a similar peasant in India who earned his living by supplying farm produce to the nearby town.

Most of the village homes were two-roomed houses shared by two families. In the outer room there was an earthen cooking stove for each family. The living room had two kangs, or earthen platforms, along the wall on opposite sides, which served as the living quarters of each family. Over each kang was knitted straw matting. During the day all the family's possessions, clothes and bedding were stacked neatly at one end. At night it became a bed for the whole family to sleep on, and in winter it could be warmed from underneath.

It was evident that the leveling-out had meant some increases in the standard of living for many. Increases in production were claimed but it must be remembered that during the war years Chinese agricultural production had gone down by about 30 per cent. The district official gave us many figures of production increases but the claims made in Peking for the country as a whole, which were lower, have perhaps more reality than what was being estimated in the villages. One or two leading villagers who had been asked to go around with us spoke of conditions before liberation and after liberation. But much of their narration compared merely the war years and the present. New China's history of records does not go back beyond 1946–47.

I visited another village about fifteen miles from Mukden in the Northeast. The Northeast was the first to carry out land reform some four years ago and as such could be expected to exhibit the maximum results of the policy. In the Northeast village was the most significant evidence of the development of New China. I saw material changes in the seven months between my two visits.

As usual when we reached the village, the villagers received us with warmth of affection, and this time they remained with us and freely mixed with us during the whole visit. Many of the men were in white shirts and blue trousers with khaki pullovers. Some of them wore old felt hats. They were taller than the peasants in the South and tougher. Almost all the women were dressed in blue garments. They offered us eggs, corn on the cob and boiled peanuts. They insisted that we eat them or take them home with us. This welcome was rather different from what we had in the village near Peking. The Peking villagers had offered me vegetables to take back to the hotel on my first visit in October, but when I returned to them in May with the official Indian Delegation, there were no such presents.

The Northeast village was called Kao Kang, possibly after the name of the Chairman of the Northeast government. On my first visit we sat in the courtyard of one of the huts with tables and benches hurriedly brought out for our use, so that it was difficult for the district official to give us the figures of production since liberation without our questioning the peasants. On my second visit we were taken to a newly built district office about two miles away from the village where we were given all the "information." Within the village, however, we were free to mix with the peasants, enter their homes and talk to them through our interpreters.

Kao Kang had a population of 168 families or 742 persons in all. There were 2,473 mows of land; landless peasants had received as their share 2.7 mows per head while the middle peasants had about 3 mows each. Before liberation ten landlord families owning 2,413 mows had lived in the village. Today only two of these families remained and they held the same amount of land as the poor peasants. The other eight families had "left." There was no doubt that the peasant's condition had improved; he looked better fed and better clothed. But there was little to prove that the agricultural production has gone up. Whatever increase there has been is more probably due to the return to normal conditions of life after years of occupation.

The village of Kao Kang, I found on my first visit, was notable for a new experiment it was carrying out. After the distribution of land some farmers had joined in a mutual aid group. Others had formed labor exchange groups. In all there were fourteen such groups in which forty families in the village were participating, with forty men and thirteen women as members. In the mutual aid groups, labor, agricultural implements and animals brought into the pool are valued according to their age, skill and capacity and paid accordingly. In the labor exchange groups on the other hand, all labor is valued equally. I learned at last that peasants had joined one group or the other because their share of land was more than they could till with the labor available in the family. It was difficult to get this admission from the village official, who was anxious to impress on me the development of co-operative spirit in the village. But I was more interested in the reactions of the peasants directly and I persisted in questioning them one by one. Answers to my questions were often interrupted by the village official or our interpreters, and long discussions took place among them while I waited for the answer. Repeating the same question to as many persons as possible is the only way to learn the truth in a Communist country, for the answers, though similar, vary in small nuances, and gradually one learns something more than one would from parrotlike repetitions of the official handouts.

And so I found that peasants joined these groups because, since they had large families of children, they had received more land than they could work themselves. The womenfolk in such families were either ill or unavailable for field labor. I also learned that the members of a mutual aid group did not put their produce in a common pool and then divide the produce according to the value decided upon previously. Each peasant paid for the aid he had received, out of the yield of his own farm. The village official and our interpreters had said that there was a common pool but the peasants whom I questioned insisted this was not so.

The mutual aid groups were thus groups of peasants who needed to employ extra labor for which the land owner paid on the basis of agreed terms. They were in a sense employment exchanges and there was little of co-operation in the real sense of the word. I was told that such groups have been formed all over the country. In this village about a quarter of the land had come under one or the other group.

The seven months which passed between my two visits changed the face of the village. From mutual aid groups it had moved toward co-operative farming of an advanced type. Farms with defined boundaries had disappeared and in their place there was one large farm of about 450 acres. The co-operative recognized the ownership of land but only under unified management. The co-operative decided on the crops to be planted in each section and the individual farmers invested in the plan their labor, land and farm equipment. The produce was divided on an agreed basis after provision had been made for tax and seeds for the next season. Sixty per cent of the produce is allotted for labor, 30 per cent for land and 10 per cent for cattle and farm implements. Each farmer then received his share according to what he had put into the common pool.

The village had been thus able to invest in modern animal-drawn farm implements on an installment plan system sponsored by the state. The co-operative had to pay 25 per cent of the value the first year, 35 per cent the second year and the balance the third year. I was taken to the farmyard and shown the new implements, a little skeptical about the possibility of the village really owning them. I had seen very little modern equipment even on a state farm, and China certainly had little to sell to the individual villages unless such a village were an experimental site. For a moment it occurred to me that they were there only for our visit, which might or might not have been the case. It is true, however, that I could see the farming lands as one big tract, uncrisscrossed by boundaries of individual holdings. It is also true, as was admitted, that Kao Kang was the only village in the district which had gone in for co-operative farming.

This was progress in the right direction, though it is bound to create many problems of employment as and when the movement spreads over the rest of the country. If modern methods are to be used for increased production agriculture must take to large-scale farming. In China the danger is that land will be further divided from generation to generation with eventual fragmentation and diminishing returns unless the burden of population dependent on the land is transferred. The Chinese government has therefore actively promoted mutual aid farming as a first step. They are now pressing the farmer to accept co-operative farming. Collectivization will follow when they feel that they have the peasant under sufficient control so that the love of property which he evinces so deeply today will not drive him to revolt. Peng Chen, the Mayor of Peking, in his explanatory speech to the foreign visitors in October, 1951, said, "Collectivization can come only on peasant initiative. Any attempt to force the peasantry will result in the government being overthrown. The process of fragmentation has reached its limit. Now, collectivization is an economic necessity."

The peasants of the co-operative village of Kao Kang repeatedly declared their deep sense of attachment to the land which belonged to them. It was theirs, and they talked as well of the clothes they had bought and rooms they could call their own, of the pigs and chickens they bred. They spoke of the money they earned by doing subsidiary work. I heard stories of how, after the title deeds to the land had been given to them, the peasants would get up at night to look at the land and feel the joy of possession. Many Communists themselves told such stories with pride.

I visited a peasant family of three who shared a two-room hut with another family. The man was short, stocky and tough. His weatherbeaten face was deeply lined. He had been a landless peasant before land reform. Today he was a model farmer owning just under nine mows of land. His wife, who sat on the k'ang next to us, wore a blue gown and like other peasant women who had been emancipated had short hair. While she sat with folded hands, the peasant constantly referred to her for confirmation of what he was saying. Sometimes she would correct or contradict him. It appeared that she was more knowledgeable about income figures than he. Their nine-year-old daughter kept running in and out of the house. She looked rather insipid for a Chinese child, and unkempt.

For more than half an hour he told of his good fortune. "I grew millet and kaoliang in my field. Last year I was a member of a mutual aid team and as a result, I had better crops. I also bred some pigs and pulled the cart that takes the crops to the co-operative or the town. I had time to do subsidiary work and I earned more than three million yuans."

I said, "Now there is no mutual aid. You are a member of the co-operative. Will the land still belong to you?"

He looked at his wife and there was an argument be-

tween them, unintelligible to me, in which the interpreter
also joined.

Slowly and haltingly he replied, "Now I will have a
larger crop of kaoliang and millet. The land is still mine."

"But perhaps you won't be growing kaoliang any more,"
I said. "You will have to grow what the co-operative plans
to grow. Would you then think the land belongs to you?"

The farmer looked at me, a little more puzzled.

"I have put my land and my cart in the co-operative and
we will probably grow kaoliang and millet again. The land
is mine and so is the cart. I am told I will receive a share for
my cart. I will get more than last year."

"Do you like to work for others?" I asked him again.
"During mutual aid you only paid or received payment for
the work you did for somebody else, and the land remained
with you. Today where is the boundary of your land?"

"Mutual aid was good. I received help in my work. I will
earn still more from the co-operative. I have only invested
my land and my cart. The land is mine."

There is enthusiasm for work and obvious pride in the
improvement of his lot but there is also determination to
continue to possess what has been acquired after centuries
of suffering. The People's Government of China is conscious of this limitation on all their plans for collectivization
of the land. The crucial question is whether they will succeed in the near future in persuading the peasant to give up
his property for the common good or whether they will be
compelled to use force.

3

HUAI RIVER PROJECT

ALONG the broad expanse of the Huai, the river barge wended its tortuous way slowly and languidly. Three rivers, the Huai, the Yangtze and the Yellow, sweep the vast plains of China's heartland, nourishing the soil and often bringing deep sorrow to the millions who depend upon them. The ancient people who have lived here for centuries had known a gentle art of living in the midst of misery and poverty which still exist today. But now a new wind is sweeping over them, gathering up the dust of ages and uncovering the human soul in search of happiness.

I have felt the vigor of a people who were fashioning their life anew, sensed the enthusiasm of youth marching to the beat of the new songs and saw their heroic determination to work and to build. But to what ultimate aim, one wonders. Is freedom from hunger all that a man needs? What use is it to have a satisfied stomach, if your mind cannot soar and reach out the uncharted universe, if your eyes cannot see new forms and new beauty? I cannot answer the question for I have not known hunger. But I know hunger is the law of the jungle.

THE GREAT PEACE

Here on the Huai and in the rest of the country, far away from Peking, one could see some of the millions who made up this great country and learn something of the problems which afflict them. They were all around us, living and toiling on their junks or on their small fields. They worked as no other people in this world work. Little children marched along the banks with their small bodies bent across a wooden bar tied to the end of the rope, which was towing the junk up the river. A man and his child pulled the plow across the field whose produce meant life or death to the village beyond. This was China and it will remain so unless the revolution succeeds in untying the yoke that binds these millions to poverty.

For a thousand years and more the Chinese peasants had carried their heavy burdens with little hope. The land was fertile and the mighty rivers brought both nourishment and a challenge. Living in isolation, they had cut themselves away from the transforming processes of the world outside. Society remained stagnant while men clung to the past which gave them peace and security. Dynasties came and went, but the Chinese peasant remained apathetic and unconcerned, bound by ancestor worship, filial piety and the Confucian obedience to the ruler. Buddhism, which swept over the country in the fourth and fifth centuries A.D., was not able to change the life of the people. Buddha, the prince seeking self-nirvana, became the God of infinite light strengthening the austere ethics of Confucianism, which called upon the people to sacrifice at the altar of their ancestors. The monarch was the supreme father of the nation. The millions of Chinese remained on the land, enslaved to the feudal landlords in whom all the political authority was vested, and unable to free themselves from outworn customs and traditions.

But New China has transformed all this. The peasant has been released from the shackles of the past and the whole society is in the process of transformation. As Jack Belden says, "The story of the upsetting of land relations in China is a rich cross-section of a new epoch that has dawned in an ancient land." I could feel the new joy of the peasant in the little bit of land he possessed, his intense pride and his faith in the Communist Party which had made this change possible. He walked with his back unbent and his eyes sparkled as he looked straight at you. His wife and daughter too shared in the glory. They were no longer shut up in the home cowering to hide their bodies from the lustful eye of the village lord. There was no incense burning in the temples before an inscrutable Buddha attended by saffron-robed priests. New China had emerged with new men in charge of her destiny. It must have been a hard task to break the solid crust of ages.

This earth held much passion for the millions of China. It was easy to see why it was so. As I sat on the barge on this wet spring day, a cold and chilly wind was blowing across the plains of this limitless horizon. The landscape was curved while the watery rope that was the river twined around holding the little pieces of earth together. Even the passing of this little barge set up ripples that changed the contours of the earth. The land, while it remained firm, brought life and hope. The peasant therefore clung to it out of his love of life and fear of death. He could stand on its firmness and fight for it. The land was the be-all and the end-all for him. His life has changed but I doubt if his attitude could change enough to make him

conscious of what was happening beyond the limits of his
village. He has always lived for the day. He has never had
faith in all the tomorrows which the politician or the priest
are so anxious to promise. He has wanted to be left alone.
And now that he has found his beloved earth again, what
else could he wish for? Four thousand years ago, an anony-
mous Chinese poet wrote:

> From break of day,
> Till sunset glow,
> I toil.
> I dig my well
> I plow my field
> And earn my food
> And drink.
> What care I
> Who rules the land
> If I
> Am left in Peace.

For centuries the Chinese peasant had been left alone to
the avarice of the local landlord, but now he could be alone
only at the risk of overturning the society which his rulers
were working to evolve. He was being called upon to
march in processions, wave the five-starred red flag, learn
his duties as a small cog in the giant wheel of communism
which was slowly but surely turning. He must be prepared
to shoulder many other tasks for what was called the common good. I have seen him and his whole family marching
for hours singing the song of "Mao Tse-tung and Stalin,"
holding out his few crumpled, soiled notes of people's currency as a "voluntary contribution" to the Aid Korea and
Resist America Fund with apparent joy in return for the
land which he now possessed. He has taken up the gun to

join the People's Liberation Army. He is under an obligation, and every time he gazes at his field, he picks up a little clod of earth, feels its small grains in his hands and is stirred once again by love and joy. He would do anything for the men who had given him back his land. But how long will this sense of obligation last? The farmer is by nature an individualist but he can no longer be left alone.

I was here on the Huai to witness the massive sense of possession which I was told had moved more than two million men and women to come forward and help in a project to save the millions inhabiting this valley. It was a multipurpose project to harness the great rivers which had acquired the unenviable name of China's great sorrow. With us on the barge was the Deputy Chief Engineer, a woman who was in charge of the whole project. In Peking, I had met many women holding important positions in the government. There were the Minister of Health, the Assistant Minister of Justice and many others who were shining examples of China's liberated womanhood. They strode about in drab Sun Yat-sen suits of poor quality blue cotton cloth, their hair brushed back and held taut by two bobby clips. No cosmetics highlighted their ivory skins. They were grim, earnest and stridently aggressive.

Even the three women interpreters, Kanpus, petty officials of the Foreign Office who accompanied the Delegation, took themselves seriously and seldom permitted themselves to smile. They were petite, dressed in cotton suits with the top coat buttons open so that the faded whiteness of their simple shirts relieved the ugliness of the dusty blue garments. Their faces were pale and grim and their straight hair, brushed tautly back and held by two bobby pins, gave them an earnest intense look. Occasionally one of them would wear a colored silk scarf as a reminder that the women of China still love their beautiful silks and gay colors. I remember the interpreter who had accompanied me on my previous visit to China as a serious young woman who never showed interest in clothes or simple diversions. I asked her once if she wouldn't like to wear attractive clothes. Her reply was pert and prompt, "We will wear nice clothes when our country is able to afford them." In Shanghai once I was feeling a little happy and gay, and so I turned to her and hummed a dance tune, knowing the Chinese enjoyed dancing. I met a cold stare and was gently reminded that China did not like bourgeois sentiments. I was reduced to silence. The proverbial gentleness and femininity of woman existed no longer in China. A revolution must harden even a soft heart or else it will fail.

But this woman engineer was a dominating personality. She had under her authority thousands of men whom she organized and controlled. She had the confidence and the consciousness of power of an old Party associate, for Chien Chin-yeng had joined the Communists in 1941 in Shanghai as a student and escaped to the liberated area in 1942 to fight against the Japanese. For two days on the hundred-mile journey upstream in a tiresome barge, she held me by the force of her raucous voice. She walked about the narrow gangway with an easy shuffle, her mannish shoes sticking out under a pair of gaudy coarse red woolen socks. Her blue cotton trousers were bunched up at the waist and unusually short at the ankles. She was obviously respected and admired by the staff, for they clustered around her and listened to her with fawning eyes. There was nothing pretty about her. Her high-cheekboned face, straight hair, and protruding teeth and broad mouth arrested your attention because of her unhesitating self-assurance. There was a twinkle of laughter and anger which alternately showed in her eyes. Because of the self-convinced arrogance of her Communist faith, she was more than a plain woman or an engineer, and I was fascinated.

For seven hours one day, with breaks for lunch and tea, she spoke of technical and other details concerning the Huai River project. "For nine years under the reactionary Kuomintang, the people of this region suffered terrible floods," she said. "Five million people died. It is only under the leadership of Mao Tse-tung and the Communist Party that an honest effort could be made to avert such disaster. In 1938 the reactionaries breached the dikes on the Yellow River, which then changed its course and flowed into the Huai. The Huai in turn was thus silted up and the region between the Yellow and the Huai became one vast lake."

Hatred for the "reactionaries" could easily be aroused in the minds of the ignorant by statements such as this, which unashamedly suppressed the facts. What interested me particularly was the attempt to impress a group of visitors who could be expected to be familiar with the recent history of China. We were to hear such versions of history too often, and it was necessary to remain vigilant always if we were to form correct judgments of what we were told. Actually, 935 floods and droughts since the fourteenth century had afflicted the people who lived along this usually serene river. They called her the "Young Maiden" and loved her as no other river was loved. "Wherever we go, no matter how far we go, there is no place like Huai," they sang, but she brought much sorrow and many calamities. The welfare of fifty million people was tied up in this valley. It was one of the most thickly populated areas of China and its reclamation offered an opportunity to any government anxious to strike deep roots of sympathy in the people. The Communists seized upon it, in 1949, immediately after the declaration of the Republic. Mao Tse-tung announced, "The Huai must be harnessed."

The Huai River undertaking reveals all the strength and weaknesses of present-day China, the wealth of man power and the paucity of technical skill. The Chinese peasant had year after year worked to maintain the system of dikes and canals. Once the dikes were breached, the river ruined her own bed, silted it up and flooded the countryside. The peasant stood by, victim of his own helplessness. Any attempt to rebuild the dikes required the mobilization of peasantry in their millions. And the Communists succeeded in doing it. Fifty thousand Communist party members and 100,000 youth leaders were spread over the districts to activate and mobilize the people. Meetings, slogans and processions were organized, and young peasants, victims of the Japanese or the local landlords, were put on the platform to remind the people that the government had given them the land. It was now their turn to work harder than the cadres who worked for them. "Happiness through hardship," "sweetest through bitterest," the peasant was repeatedly told, and he listened.

Chou-shan was a rural worker forty-eight years old, tough of body and hard-working. The previous winter he went with one of the Huai River propagandists on a tour of the villages to mobilize workers for the project. At a meeting of the peasants he said, "In the past we were taxed heavily. We worked on the river only to protect the lands of the landlords. Now Mao has given us the land, my family has received twenty-one mows of land. We must therefore work on the Huai River and protect our own land."

Chin Shu-ling was a daughter of a poor peasant whose father was killed by the Japanese when she was only nine years old. Under land reform she was given some land. Her main task was to mobilize women and men of her village. She and many others like her who had been victims of the Kuomintang and landlord oppression had now become active propagandists for the new regime. With their help, 2,200,000 men and women were drafted to labor, often with their own spades, during their off-season between the autumn harvest and the spring sowing. They were given free accommodation, medical care and 4 catties (1 catty = 1.1 pound) of rice as their daily wages. They worked on the average for eighty days during the year. During the last two years they have rebuilt 1,370 miles of dikes and dredged 540 miles of river bed.

But it was not enough to reopen the river course. The flow of the water must be controlled and the water conserved. There are some two hundred tributaries which empty their water in the Huai. These are to be controlled by building twenty-one reservoirs in the mountain region where these tributaries originate. A dam is already built in the middle valley for the purpose of reducing the flow from 13,000 cubic yards to 6,500 cubic yards per second. Further storage capacity will be increased by regulating and deepening seventeen lakes including the great Hung-cha Lake in the middle and lower reaches of the river. The plan implies as well the building of dams, sluices and culverts, and it requires technical skill and equipment. It is stated that about 16,000 technical men, which includes foremen as well as students and top engineers, are engaged on the project together with some 40,000 administration cadres. It is difficult to believe these figures, for China does not have trained personnel in such large numbers to spare on a single project. There is, however, a tendency in Chinese industry to consider a "model worker" as almost an engineer, and at the end of 1950 there were some 24,672 model workers elected from the men working on the Huai project.

Chin-yeng, the woman deputy engineer, is herself not a qualified engineer. She had been a student in the third year of the engineering faculty of Shanghai University before she escaped to the liberated area. But while I listened to her talk on the barge, I was under her spell and did not realize that all the talk of a multipurpose project was more propaganda than reality. I was to realize it only after seeing the "dam" at Junghochi, which is supposed to be the main structure of what will ultimately be the central control of the Huai River valley.

This journey upstream was full of many disappointments. But it also contained a vital lesson for an Indian. A project which seeks to irrigate about eight million acres of land, directly benefit seventeen million people and bring safety to some fifty million more must appear gigantic in its proportions. Besides the local population involved, the number of men and women it claimed to mobilize for its speedy accomplishment made the project perhaps the biggest talking point in favor of the New Democracy of China. I was therefore not the only person who was anxious to see it. The Indian Delegation which I was accompanying was eager to learn the lessons that might usefully be applied to many similar problems which face Indians today. The Delegation was being taken one hundred miles up the river at the special request of the Prime Minister of China. It was told that no other visitors had been taken so far to see the construction work. Despite the many inconveniences of the small barge, they pursued the journey with avid interest. It was, however, to prove a fruitless trip.

We passed many villages along the banks but they seemed to be leading their daily humdrum life. There were no signs of tremendous activity. The work on the dikes was finished, or so it appeared, and the river was contained in her bed. Occasionally we saw a children's procession carrying the red banner. But it was a silent routine march. There were no songs or slogans. Even the three nights we slept on the barge were unmarked by the beat of drums and the chime of cymbals which announce the farmers dancing Yang-ko.

Yang-ko had been an old peasant dance which had been once suppressed by rural puritanism. Mao had revived it and given it his personal approval, and it accordingly became a part of the cultural movement sponsored by the Communists. Men, women and children danced in the cities and the villages to express "the People's urge to be free and to laugh once again." It is a folk dance originally connected with the harvest time and is danced without any specific partner either in a circle or in a kind of conga line. The music is provided by cymbals and small drums hanging waist high from the dancers' necks. The rhythm is simple and easy to follow but is monotonously repetitious. One of the old songs which the Chinese sang while dancing the Yang-ko was:

> Harvest every year; but yearly—nothing,
> Borrow money yearly; yearly still in debt,

Broken huts, small basins, crooked pots;
Half an acre of land, five graves!

Five graves for the farmer Chin's family and half an acre
of land! He still has only half an acre of land. The Yang-ko
is now a dance for the whole year, danced in October 1st
parades and at the picnics of school children.

But now it was spring on the Huai and the farmer was
too busy to dance. Apart from a solitary old-fashioned
dredger clanking its chains as it scooped up the silt I saw
nothing. Life seemed to go on unstirred by the great purpose of harnessing the "young maiden." But I remained
hopeful that perhaps at the great dam of Junghochi we
would see something of the moving enthusiasm which had
moved millions to attempt to conquer what seemed to be
insurmountable difficulties with bare human hands.

We passed innumerable junks carrying their load of men,
women and children. They drifted along the river to no
apparent purpose. The tiny tattered junk was for many of
them their only home. It will be a long time before the
teeming millions of China will find a stable life and a roof
over their withered bodies. After forty-eight hours of slow
and tiresome journey, we arrived at Junghochi, hoping to
see the accomplishments and share the enthusiasm of New
China. But once again, it eluded us.

I looked at the sight with baffled surprise. So much had
been said about this project and its completion in three
months' time last year through "the strength and the intelligence of the masses of people." We saw before us not a
dam but a simple three-part *anicut* or obstruction built
across the river to control the water's flow. The first section was the open river bed; the second section, three
hundred yards long, had eight sluice gates; and the third

section, with four sluice gates, diverted the waters to low-lying fields which were called the lake area. Despite the formidable statistics of men and material used, here was something so simple that I felt I did not want to look at it. Our guide and host, the Deputy Chief Engineer, saw the obvious disappointment on my face. There were no enthusiastic millions of rural workers, nor any evidence that they could once have been housed here for three months. A few hutments stood in the lake area and that was all. Even the construction of the third section was not complete, and the whole theory of flood control seemed to be to flood the less fertile upper regions of the river and thus free the middle valley. The Deputy Chief admitted this, but she defended the approach on the ground that the lower region was more fertile than the area now coming under floods. Her pride was hurt, but she tried to maintain it by pointing out that the entire dam was the work of the Chinese people. "The sluice gates, the concrete mixers and everything that we needed," she asserted, "were made in China. We have spent money equivalent to 1,350,000 tons of rice. We are going to build the lock on the open river later." Work was now going on further upstream at Futzling, she added, and if I were interested in seeing China at work I should have gone there. As is usual in Communist countries, what is of interest is generally out of one's reach. One must instead be content with what is offered in innumerable official statements and handouts.

The visit to Junghochi on the Huai was nonetheless helpful. It gave silent proof of the fact that the land reform had ironed out many problems which baffle river valley projects in other countries. The question of compensation and resettlement of peasants removed from catchment areas offered no difficulties. Such peasants could be given a share in the distribution of the land somewhere else.

There was also a realistic approach to the immediate problems. China was content to seek remedies which lay within the scope of technical skill and equipment available to her. She was able to mobilize her vast man power and make it work. Without the labor of millions, the Huai dikes could not have been built within the period required. I missed, however, the feeling of the moving force behind the great upheaval which it is claimed is changing the face of this ancient land. Official publications describe the change in the outlook of the peasant as resulting from the land reform "which for the first time gave them land of their own, free of both rents and debt." The peasant, they state, now knows that he is toiling for himself and this change is essential to the constructive effort to industrialize China. I have seen this new sense of ownership enthusing the peasant in the villages we visited elsewhere. The land for him has been a symbol of hope between life and death and hope can move mountains of difficulties which beset China. But love of possession and of the common good of socialism are two different emotions.

4

WORKERS AND "MODELS"

"It was passion and principally passion," Jack Belden
writes, "that overwhelmed Chiang Kai-shek. The radiant
hopes and murderous hates that the Chinese peasantry
poured into the sphere of war and revolution released a
flood of emotional energy that exploded with the force of
an atomic bomb within Chinese society, nearly dissolving
it." World War II had unleashed these passions of the tradi-
tionally apathetic peasantry driven by utter despair and
hatred of their overlords. Their cry, "Down with the landlords who drink our blood!" was taken up by the Communists, who had hitherto advocated only rent reductions.
The Communists rode to power on the crest of the promise
to abolish landlordism and redistribute the land among the
peasants.

The revolution in China was entirely an agrarian revolution. It is to be expected, therefore, that the peasant influence would dominate the state. The Communist theory
of class struggle conceives of the working-class leadership
and dictatorship as the essential factor in the building-up of
socialism. The Chinese proletariat, which numbered about

two million industrial workers, was weak though potentially most revolutionary. The Communist Party must aim, therefore, at strengthening the working class against a peasantry which is essentially individualistic and conservative. The peasant, his land hunger satisfied, wants to be left alone in peace. It is this conflict between the worker and the peasant which will one day decide the future of communism in China.

The Communists are aware of this contradiction and have accordingly left the peasantry in possession of the land. In earlier chapters, we have seen the slow and cautious steps being taken toward co-operative agriculture. Meanwhile, by constantly reminding the people of the leadership of the working class and building up an ideologically strong and united proletariat, the Communist Party is preparing for an open and avowed dictatorship.

The labor movement in China is a vital instrument of the government. It receives material help and many other facilities from the Party. In return, the working class is expected to carry out the policies of the government, and to consolidate the power of the Communist Party which controls them. Under the Trade Union Law, the responsibility of seeing that all laws and regulations concerning the workers are strictly carried out by industry is put upon the unions. They take part in management and production directly through factory administrative committees in state-owned industry. This has brought all the workers under the control of unions though technically they are free to join the union or not, as they choose. Today, the All-China Federation of Labor has more than six million members, including workers in all the industries, post and telegraph, rail and sea transport, education, press and printing.

The factory administrative committees have been introduced to give the workers what is called the right of democratic management. In the public-owned factory, however, the committee is under the Government Industrial Administrative Bureau and is mainly concerned with the drive to speed up production. Production plans and other directives are handed down by the government bureau and the committee is required to see that such plans are carried out. The committee does little apart from what it is dirctly told to do by the state in regard to wages and other matters for the worker's welfare. There are instances in which, after a private industry had been taken over by the state, the workers have been made to accept a reduction in wages. In the privately owned industries, these committees have led to much conflict. In Shanghai many industrialists reported that interminable discussions in such meetings wasted considerable time without achieving any results. Wages, retrenchment of superfluous staff and other difficulties continue and the Government Labor Bureau to whom such disputes are referred always intervenes on the side of the workers. Often these same disputes are settled immediately to the employer's favor, once the industry is taken over by the state. Management's rights to adjust wages, allocate work, dismiss workers and regulate production exist only on paper, and many privately owned industries, other than textiles, are suffering from steadily dwindling profits because the costs of production bear little relation to prices regulated by other considerations.

The trade unions are the agencies through which the economic and political purposes of the government are effectively carried out. According to the official guide to China the activities of the All-China Federation of Labor include "emulation campaigns in the movement for increased production, improvement of safety measures and health conditions in industry, and the establishment of cultural places and clubs, with the aim of gradually eliminating illiteracy among the workers and helping the workers to study Marxism-Leninism and Mao Tse-tung's theory of the Chinese revolution."

The war in Korea has been utilized to compel the workers to work longer hours and donate extra time for the Aid Korea Fund by entering into "Patriotic Pacts." Many factories have been working an extra hour or two daily. The workers do not have an eight-hour day but a ten- or eleven-hour day. At Nanking, I heard the whistle blow to signal the end of the working day at the fertilizer factory, but no workers came out to return to their homes. They remained in the factory and sat around machines in groups of ten or twelve, discussing, I was told, "problems of production." I saw many in these groups listlessly looking around or pretending to listen to the political education that was being offered. In every factory, such classes were being held for one hour in the morning and one hour in the evening after the working hours. In these classes the workers were taught reading and were reminded of "the responsibilities of the working-class leadership." Skilled workmen were also called upon to demonstrate the handling of machinery. One could recognize the usefulness of such classes but the long hours enforced on the workers must have less advantageous results.

China Reconstructs writes:

The Chinese worker now feels a new zest for life. He knows

that he is the master of his country. In the factory he has had the practical experience of the fact that every step in increasing production is a step forward in his earnings and general welfare. Instead of being docile and passive, he now exhibits initiative.

But the initiative has been provided far more by the political campaigns which have been carried on from time to time. During the last two years there have been three campaigns in which the working class has been called upon to play the leading part, and they have been so managed as to stir up the feelings of class struggle. The first concerned itself with the weeding out of Kuomintang reactionaries; then came the Aid Korea and Resist America and finally the San Fan Wu Fan movements. In addition to the economic and financial motives behind these campaigns, they helped to rouse the workers and give them the feeling of active participation in the state as its leading class.

Another use of the labor movement as a means of increasing production was provided by the system of electing "model workers" in every plant or construction activity, and granting them many privileges including higher wages. Such model workers were always present when visitors came to see the factory, proudly showing off their medals and decorations. Many "inventions" and claims of high production were displayed in their name. They received a good deal of publicity and were sent to Peking or elsewhere to march on May Day and in other parades on special occasions. I saw many of them in the course of my visits to the plants, quietly smiling in their rather new but crumpled blue suits, awkwardly conscious of their privileges.

I do not know what actual achievements qualified a

worker for election as a "model" for I never saw any real evidence of the claims made on their behalf. These fulsome claims and the liberal use of the word "invention" defied the usual belief that technical skill grows slowly even under guidance. Perhaps the knowledge that they are not working for the capitalists "but for themselves and for the good of the whole nation" has released a flood of talent, and geniuses are springing up on every corner. In keeping with this is *China Reconstructs'* report:

When the Tientsin Automobile Assembly Plant decided to make its first car, instead of just putting cars together, it was found that many tools were lacking. The workers talked this over and improvised what was needed out of old machines and spare parts.

The car that I saw exhibited in Tientsin was the product of this "invention."

I could see in the textile industry the actual results of such "inventions." There is shortage of cloth so a national hero had to be built up who by his work methods promised plenty in the future. The story of Ho Chien-hsiu is therefore provided. It concerns a living person who has reaped her reward by her achievements in the textile industry and, according to *People's China* of April 11, 1952, runs thus:

Shantung is also the home of the nationally famous seventeen-year old Tsingtao model textile worker, Ho Chien-hsiu, who succeeded in cutting the proportion of cotton wasted in spinning on the spindles she tends from 1.5 per cent to .25 per cent. Her method has been introduced as standard throughout the country's textile industry. When universally used, it will increase production annually by 44,460 bales of yarn or 64 million yards of cloth without a penny of additional investment in machines or raw materials. These extra textiles are sufficient for the use of four million people a year at China's present rate of per capita consumption.

China Reconstructs of May-June, 1952, continues her career:

Since her achievement became known, Ho Chien-hsiu has been the recipient of many high honors. She was sent as a workers' representative to the November session of the Chinese People's Political Consultative Conference in Peking, taking part in the proceedings with national leaders in all fields. She was also elected a model member of the New Democratic Youth League. But her greatest satisfaction comes from the fact that her method is being successfully applied on an industry-wide basis and that it represents a resounding victory over conservatism.

I was able to see what this new method which had won national fame had yielded at the Hengyuan textile mills. Pien Shih-ching was the only one who gave actual statistics of production. Before liberation the Hengyuan mill employed 1,000 workers. Today it employs 1,800 and works two shifts, of ten hours each. Before liberation, the production was .64 pounds of yarn per spindle and 47.16 yards of cloth per loom per day. Now the mill produces .97 pounds of yarn per spindle and 83 yards per loom per twenty-hour day. These statistics indicate that the efficiency of the Chinese worker is at best equal to, if not less than, the Indian textile worker.

Since, in a workers' state, the worker labors both for himself and for the state, I was interested in the wages in various industries. It is not the function of the unions to act as a means of joint bargaining with management. The state has fixed the minimum wage as the cost of living for two adults, paid on a piecework basis. It was difficult to obtain clear information on what was included in the cost of living. In Mukden where the wages are paid on the basis of points assigned to such necessities as rice flour, oil, cloth, salt and coal, the point was valued at 1,900 yuans or 8 cents. On the Huai River project the peasant workers were paid 4 catties, or pounds, of rice plus free housing, but I was told that out of this wage, the peasants required 3½ catties for food, so only ½ cattie could be exchanged for other needs. The wages in factories I visited in Manchuria ranged between $8.50 minimum to $25.60 maximum per month for workers, while the model workers, now classified as "technicians," were paid about $41. In Tientsin, in the textile mill, the workers' wages were in terms of millet and worked out to about $28 a month. These wages are comparable to what is received in the Indian textile industry.

The wages are low in the heavy industries in Mukden. I did hear in Shanghai, however, that as soon as the factory was taken over by the state, the union agreed to lower the wages as the workers' contribution to the government's economy drive. It is a fact that the present wages in China represent an increase both in cash and real value. In addition, the Labor Insurance Regulations, passed in March, 1951, give considerable protection against old age and sickness.

Under the law, management is called upon to bear the medical expenses and pay the wages of workers on sick leave. Workers receive full pay for three months for occupational injuries and half pay for nonoccupational injuries. For a further period of three to six months they receive one-third to one-half pay from the insurance fund. After this they can draw a disability pension. Retirement pensions are given from the insurance fund to men and women over the ages of sixty and fifty respectively. The qualification for such a pension is twenty-five years' service with ten years' service in the enterprise from which they retire. Women workers are paid full wages for fifty-six days for confinement, and maternity benefits from the insurance fund as well. The entire cost of labor insurance is borne by the state and the employer and employee make no payments toward it. The law is applied specifically to factories of certain size though the smaller firms are expected to follow the example as far as possible.

The unions together with management have also set up rest homes, sanatoriums and nurseries. In the factories, cheap cafeterias provide a diet suited to the work done there. There are no leaves of absence and a worker is not allowed to stay away on grounds other than illness. There is also no dismissal from a job. I have referred to the difficulties of retrenchment felt by the foreign firms, but this common rule does avoid what would otherwise be a serious problem of unemployment in the working class. They cannot return to the land as the peasantry is already under-employed.

Such a policy is possible because the production costs are no consideration in the Communist economy. It was difficult to obtain any idea of costs in any of the factories I visited, and possibly no such figures are maintained. As the country is short of all manufactured goods, the prices of manufactured articles are adjusted instead to the necessity of controlling consumption and maintaining a stable economy. Wages, too, were determined, I was told by the manager of a Mukden factory, by "the general productive conditions of the whole country as directed by the government." This implied that they were fixed once again ac-

cording to permitted limits of consumption and not by prevailing conditions in the particular industry, as is usual in a
capitalist economy.

It was evident in every factory I visited that the workers
feel a new sense of ownership and are conscious of the fact
that they are the leading class in the nation composed of a
working class, peasantry, bourgeoisie and national capitalists. In every political and economic activity in the country
the worker is pushed to the foreground and reminded of
his duty to lead the Chinese people toward socialism. Here
is a story how this consciousness was expressed during the
inquisition of commercial houses that occurred during the
Wu Fan purge in 1952. It was the examination of Chen
Tsung-shen of the China Toothbrush Company, by a
seventeen-year-old apprentice representing the workers, as
reported in Chinese newspapers:

Question: What does an apprentice do?

Answer: Learn a craft.

Question: Why should he be beaten then?

Answer: This is my mistake.

Question: What should be done?

Answer: To subject myself to the leadership of the working class and to lower my head to the workers.

Question: Why did you hand your confession to the
government and why does the government transfer it
to us?

Answer: Because you are the leading class in the country.

Question: Yes! then what kind of a person are you?

Answer: I am a bad merchant.

Question: Are you a criminal?

Answer: Yes.

Thus the passion of the people is aroused by skillful propaganda and promises of the millennium to come. Such promises are made real by intensely promoting a sense of possession and fomenting hatreds against those who appear to prevent the possession of the object desired. Hope is further kindled with the help of living "models." Even as a casual visitor in China I could sense this emotion in the Chinese worker. He is known for his capacity to work hard and lift heavy burdens, but today, he works with hope. He is no longer apathetic. He wants to learn the job he is doing, and to read and write. Enthusiasm alone cannot teach him to handle the machine or obtain for him a new one. He does not realize China cannot reach the goal she seeks by the methods she is following.

5

FOREIGN AID

Any estimate of China's industrial effort today must take into consideration the existing foreign industrial establishments, the possibilities of their future expansion through further investments and the availability of local technical skill. It is an accepted fact that there was little, if any, effort to industrialize the country and develop her vast resources in the past. Except for the few industrial centers along the coastal belt, most of the vast hinterland remained a rural area, producing raw materials for export and dependent upon imports for such manufactured goods as were needed.

The few industries which developed were mostly concerned with the manufacture of such essential goods as cloth, soap and cigarettes, and mining and public utilities such as transport, water supply and electricity. Many of these enterprises were owned and managed by the foreigners who came to China lured by a huge home market and the possibilities of unchecked exploitation. Large profits accumulated and were taken out of the country while the Chinese people had no say about prices, wages or the fiscal policy of their country which could arrest their exploitation. The foreign interests found human beings cheap. The Chinese say that the foreign investors recouped their original capital investments twice or thrice within a few years.

In such a situation a wise government sees as its primary function the improvement of its people's standard of living. There can be no other paramount consideration, other than the maintenance of the country's freedom and integrity. But the Communists in China, as elsewhere, seek power and domination and not the betterment of the people. It was very easy to turn the sorrow of the millions into a bitter anger against the foreigner who had heaped many indignities upon a gentle and quiet people. Even such anger would be worth while if the dynamic energy it released could replace the skill, the knowhow and the capital necessary for a constructive effort. Unfortunately the little that I have seen in China does not warrant such hope.

The effort to industrialize is solely preoccupied in reconstructing what little can be done without capital equipment and technical guidance. There would still be hope if China could supply the necessary skill through her workers and engineers. But even in this direction she is badly handicapped.

China's economic development was limited from the start by lack of transport. The railroads run from north to south along the coastal areas, and the hinterland remains cut off from the rest of the country. Only the rivers provide east to west traffic. There are about twelve thousand miles of railroad, originally managed by four powers—Britain, Japan, France and China—in the entire country. It is true that China's railroads are today efficiently managed. Through traffic is provided from north to south over an integrated system. It is also true that many of the public utilities such as water supply and electric power supply, which have been taken over from foreign concerns in places such as Shanghai, are ably administered contrary to fears expressed in some quarters. But the industrial plants are poorly equipped and lack technical guidance and managerial ability, because the necessary personnel is not available. Even the universities and technical institutions are not in a position to supply this want in the near future.

I visited practically all the famous universities in China and saw the many handicaps from which they suffer. There is little equipment for practical training and the sudden elimination of English texts has left these institutions with hardly any books in Chinese for educational use. The country's need is so great that students are drafted into jobs immediately on finishing their education. The universities are preoccupied in solving immediate problems or manufacturing spare parts for some industry. They are thus unable to give a general technical training or prepare the students in fields other than those presently in demand.

It is often reported that China has received considerable technical assistance and that there are thousands of Russian technicians in China, helping her to rebuild her war-torn economy. It is difficult to learn the exact number, but everything indicates that the Russian technicians are inadequate in number to provide all the assistance China needs. I saw some Russians living in the hotels I stayed at in Peking, Mukden and Tientsin. They left the hotel early in the morning, ate their meals in separate dining rooms and kept to themselves. They went in cars specially reserved for them. Often such cars moved about the city with dark curtains drawn across their windows. I was told that these people were technical advisers to the Chinese government, were organized into a military corps of engineers and were working in bureaus appointed to supervise particular industries. They were under strict discipline and received a small salary plus board and lodging. Throughout my two visits to China, I never came across any of them in an industrial plant. But at the headquarters of the Huai River Harnessing Committee at Pang Pu, I saw a painting in which the Russian water conservation expert, Bukoff, was shown discussing the plans with the Chinese staff in charge of the project.

All the factories that I visited appeared to be working under Chinese management without day-to-day technical supervision or guidance. The Russians came in only when a problem arose which the Chinese could not solve and only when such problems were referred to the bureau concerned.

Old China had other sources of aid which the new government could have utilized if it had so desired. Japan, Britain, the United States and many other powers had large sums invested in industries in China. The Japanese investments were taken over after the defeat of Japan. The United States investments were put under strict control in retaliation for the freezing of Chinese assets in the United States. But Britain still remained. Estimates set the British investments in trade and industry in China at 200 million pounds in 1930. There were considerable additional investments before the war. Today, in terms of present valuation, the investments must be worth much more than 350 million pounds.

These British firms were ready and anxious to do business with China. They were administered by men who had been old China hands, who had lived in the country for twenty years and more and knew it well. Many of them may have had contempt for the people of the country or a white man's burden complex, but they were businessmen anxious to seize a chance to make profits. And they were powerful enough to make Britain maintain a friendly policy toward China.

The Britishers had therefore remained behind, in the hope that the Chinese would sooner or later realize the value and necessity of doing business with them. They rightly believed China needed many essential consumer goods, machinery, technical guidance and capital and they were willing to supply them if they could retain their investments and were allowed to make legitimate profits. They therefore waited and hoped.

Perhaps the Englishmen were justified in their hope. The difficulties China faced were apparent to anyone who knew even a little about the country. Realizing them, the new government had accepted the capitalist as a necessary element in its society. Mao Tse-tung wrote: "To develop industry enormous capital is required. Where will it come from? It can come from only two sources: the capital accumulated by the Chinese people themselves and from foreign loans, and we shall welcome all foreign investments as long as they obey the laws of China and are advantageous to our economy." He had again repeated this in *People's Democratic Dictatorship*, "We want to do business transactions and we certainly do not oppose anyone else." In 1951, Chou En-lai could still say in reply to my question, "Of course we welcome very much any assistance from friendly countries."

So the British industrialist remained, hoping to do business. China has a long memory and still carries the effects of the burden of the past; but while it may be difficult for an individual to forget the bitter humiliation heaped upon him by the arrogance of a superiority complex, a nation conscious of its strength rises above such petty frustrations. The interests of the people demanded that China utilize any agency which offered the technical help necessary for the rapid advancement of the standard of living of the people. Industrially developed Western Europe and the United States are the only countries in a position to give this assistance in a far greater measure than the Communist countries. Measures could be adopted which would prevent any interference in the policies of the government. In any case, to reject such help because it may lead to interference is to confess the weakness of the government and the lack of faith in its capacity.

China is unable to make up her mind about the British. They offer her an open door to the Western storehouse but their past record in China has left an unhappy memory of domination and exploitation. So, while many statements are made which give hope to the foreigner, in actual fact a policy of discrimination and vengeance for the past is slowly pushing the foreigner out of China. On the eve of the British Note asking for facilities to aid the withdrawal of the British industrialists from China, Nan Han-chen, Governor of the People's Bank, said in reply to my question about the status of existing foreign interests in the country, "Existing foreign industrialists and traders may continue to operate in the country. We shall welcome foreign investments on the basis of mutual benefit and equality, provided they work within the law." The same reply was given to the British Note by the Vice-Minister of Foreign

Affairs. These statements actually have little meaning, because the foreign interests in China, though they are working within the law, are gradually but inevitably being snuffed out.

The methods adopted to carry out the process have all the artistry of a cruel sadism which revels in watching the agony of prolonged torture. The sense of property and the greed for profit have led the one-time oppressor to walk into the trap laid by the oppressed. The foreigners, who had once bled China white, are now unable to leave their possessions and depart. China feels that she is making them pay for the past.

Today many foreigners, including the British, want to leave their property and the country but unfortunately they cannot do it. I know that the owners of the world-famous Cathay Hotel wanted to abandon their property and turn it over to the Chinese, but it took their manager more than two years to settle their liabilities and adjust their accounts with the government before he could obtain a release and an exit permit. The managing director of a famous international tobacco company took almost a year to hand over the factory, and is still waiting for his exit permit. Meanwhile liabilities continue to increase, since taxes and labor who cannot be discharged have to be paid. At the same time, the responsibility for meeting such liabilities, including the responsibility for any illegal acts by members of the staff, either in the present or at any time in the past, is placed upon the manager and remains as a constant threat to personal security and freedom.

During my visit to Shanghai, I met many foreign tycoons of industry and trade. They were old China hands who since the revolution had not been able to leave the precincts of Shanghai. They therefore knew little of New China. Many of them may have retained their attitudes about the inferiority of colonial peoples but in their utter isolation they received me as a breath of fresh air with eagerness and pleasure. I knew they were dependent upon the good offices of the Indian Embassy for many things but they did not welcome me because of that. I was a journalist willing to listen to them and to speak of facts and not of fiction.

I visited them in their offices alone and unhampered. One of the industrialists confessed to me that he was surprised at the risk I was taking. I knew the Chinese who were detailed to look after me did not like my moving about. Every time I returned from an engagement, I was asked where I had been. But I continued my visits with various businessmen until my own Embassy thought it necessary to convey to me indirectly that I was embarrassing them by endangering my personal security!

While visiting one business establishment in Shanghai, I saw the fate of the private capitalist especially the foreign capitalist—painted large on the door of the manager's office. A bloated exploiter wrapped in corruption and speculation was being gored by the bayonet of a triumphant worker. This was the picture he saw every time he entered his office, and he was powerless to remove the insult.

What I saw of foreign business in Shanghai convinced me that it was not a question of mutual benefit and equality or working within the law which would enable it to continue to operate. The Chinese were determined to take back the pound of flesh, and then throw out the carcass. How this is being achieved is an interesting story because there appears to be no way to extricate the men involved in the mess.

The British Note expresses the feeling of the seven-hundred-odd Englishmen now remaining in China that they no longer hope to be able to carry on their trade or maintain their investments. The continuing world tension, the war in Korea and the policy of the Chinese government convinced them that it was time to go. Many of them told me that discriminatory taxation, inability to reduce costs and diversion of trade from private hands to the state, with a rigid policy of price control had led their firms into great difficulties. They had few funds left to meet the demands made on them. Their liability was personal and with no prospects of loans from banks on their stock, they faced a constant threat of imprisonment. I was surprised that men who had to pay nineteen shillings on the pound at home should complain of taxation in China where income tax was only 30 per cent at the most. "But we have to pay this tax," someone said to me, "whether we make profits or no profits. And generally there are no or little profits."

Foreign enterprises in China have not been permitted to carry out revaluation of their assets and stocks. Accordingly, depreciation is still being calculated on book values as of August 31, 1949, despite the fact that Hong Kong dollar rate has risen since that date by 9.7 times. Foreign firms are therefore presumed to have made large profits and are taxed at the maximum. A firm importing pianos was called upon to pay the tax though throughout the year it had not sold a single instrument. Chinese firms, on the other hand, were allowed to revalue their assets in terms of the new exchange value. The taxes are collected immediately and a fine of 1 per cent a day is imposed for every day of default.

Many factories were unable to work all year round because of the shortage of raw materials, yet they had to pay their workers for the whole period. In addition they could not dispense with any surplus labor. In theory, workers could be discharged, after prior agreement with the trade union, on payment of three months' wages. But in practice, such agreement was difficult to obtain, and even if it were reached, wages for one month for every year of service plus three months had to be paid in a flat sum. The purpose was evidently to force a firm to retain every one of its workers until it liquidated. Behind such policy was, no doubt, the constantly growing problem of unemployment of industrial and agricultural labor. Ultimately it forces the private industrialist to withdraw as no profits can be made. The prospects in China, however, are much grimmer than the mere consideration of profits. The payment for raw materials, taxes and the irreducible wage bill have to be made immediately, while stocks of finished goods accumulate and tie up the liquid assets. These liabilities could have been met, possibly, by such industries as textiles if they were given time, or if they could obtain advances from the bank. But all such requests for advances have been refused by the People's Bank. So, the foreign firm is forced to bring in fresh capital from its home country or its directors will face imprisonment, because the Chinese law imposes personal liability on the heads of a business house.

Jardine, Matheson & Co., Ltd. was virtually a business empire in Old China. Their activities included shipping, wharves and docks, textiles, engineerng, brewng and others. The brewery was working under a contract with the

Chinese government whereby its entire production was taken by the authorities. In January, 1952, as a measure in the economy drive, the government decided to cut the consumption of beer, and reduced its purchases. The result was that in March the company had thirty thousand barrels of beer in stock tying up a large amount of money. Mr Gordon, the managing director, therefore had no money to meet the company's liabilities, including wages. He asked for an advance against the millions of pounds sterling worth of assets and stocks, but the bank refused to consider it. There was no alternative other than to send for money from London or face imprisonment. Gordon refused to send for the money, for he argued the Chinese would not permit him to remit such an advance to London when he is in a position to repay it.

So the Chinese were faced with the dilemma of arresting him and destroying all future prospects of industrial and commercial co-operation with the foreign businessmen in China, or waiving the law. For twenty days they argued with Gordon. "Surely, Mr. Gordon, how can a firm like Jardine's have no money? It is only a matter of a couple of thousand pounds and you would not like us to put you in prison." For days persuasion and pressure were tried alternately, but to no avail. Ultimately, the Chinese had to arrest Gordon. This was perhaps the last straw for the very patient British, and they decided to leave China and abandon their investments worth more than 350 million pounds.

This desperate comedy was played because for the last two years the British had been forced to bring in fresh capital to save their old investments. It was estimated that in 1951 the British firms in Shanghai brought in six million pounds. In 1952 the intake had been reduced to twenty-five thousand pounds a month because of further decreases in production and demand. Gordon's arrest is a clear indication that the Chinese policy toward foreign business houses is to squeeze them out and at the same time to utilize their resources for China's own purposes without any payment.

The patience of the Britishers now in China was remarkable. They went to their offices smartly dressed, played their week-end golf and patiently waited. They had ardent faith in themselves and firmly believed China needed their services much more now than ever before. They were prepared to adjust themselves to the altered circumstances.

I had met John Keswick in Hong Kong. He was a tall, handsome Englishman who hid behind his playboy looks a sound understanding of Chinese economy. For a long time he was convinced that Britain could do business with China. Many of his friends jokingly called him "Communist." The story of his fantastic escape from Tientsin shows how slowly the bureaucratic machine works, especially when, in a country like China, the administration is still inexperienced. Keswick was in Tientsin, anxious to return to England. After long delays, he had been able to obtain his exit permit. Then someone in the Ministry of Interior must have realized that if Keswick left China there would be no one left as a hostage to compel the English firm to bring in more capital. Keswick was already aboard a British ship when a police officer approached and asked him to leave the ship and return to his bungalow. No explanations were offered for this "request."

Keswick knew that if he refused he would only be forcibly taken off the ship. So he went back to his house to await the call to the police station. On the second or third day he sent his Chinese servant to the station and asked for the return of the exit permit which, he informed the police, belonged to him legally. The police had no instructions to withdraw the exit permit so they quietly returned it to him. For a fortnight Keswick waited but no call came from the police.

Once again another British ship was due to leave Tientsin for Hong Kong. An hour before departure time, Keswick sent a note to the police telling them that he was leaving aboard the ship after having waited for a fortnight for them to seek any explanations they wanted. "I cannot," he wrote, "wait any longer and as I have an exit permit I am going." The police did not know what to do and they could not contact Peking for instructions in time. It was by sheer ability to do the right thing at the right time that Keswick was able to escape from China.

A Soviet Russia anxious to industrialize herself had done business with Britain and the United States even though they had intervened against the Bolsheviks on the side of the White Russians after World War I. Why not China? Has China such bitter memories of the past, or are other forces at work which hold sway over the future of the Chinese people and seek to prevent the rise of a prosperous New China?

6

INDUSTRY IN PROGRESS

"Unquestionably, in constructing New China, industrialization is our goal and we are exerting every effort to attain this goal," said Mr. Chen Yun, the Chairman of the Committee of Financial and Economic Affairs.

"It will in effect take three to five years to revive the economy in China before it can be developed systematically. Within this period, we should concentrate our strength on the development of several key points which will facilitate the preparation of essential conditions for industrialization such as capital, the home market and the technique," Chou En-lai stated.

These were the reports submitted to the National Committee of the People's Political Consultative Council in September, 1950. I visited Chinese industrial plants in 1951 and 1952 and so was able to see for myself what these efforts were and to what extent the promises held out have been fulfilled. China must industrialize if the poverty of her millions is to be eased. But she faces immense difficulties, many of which are today common to all underdeveloped countries. And others which are of her own making or imposed upon her by the world conflict.

China claims to have overcome some of the difficulties and asserts that she has made phenomenal progress both in industrial production and technique. At a recent industrial exhibition in India, the Chinese Pavilion exhibited machine tools and other products which impressed many visitors. Chinese newspapers and magazines announce hundreds of "inventions" her workers are manufacturing. Chinese leaders hand out statistics of great increases in industrial production to impress their people and assure them that prosperity is close at hand. Unfortunately these statistics tell nothing because, as in the case of the agricultural figures, they are merely percentage increases over 1949 and 1950.

China was once the dumping ground of the world. During the inflationary period the motley goods thus accumulated assumed the status of currency and large-scale hoarding increased the scarcity. Today, these stocks still supply the vital needs of the people as other sources of supply are closed. Shops in big cities are full of goods which were manufactured five to ten years ago. Local manufactures such as cigarettes, soap and cloth are numerous but their prices are high in an obvious effort to limit their consumption. Many medicines and drugs are old and perhaps useless.

The stability of the Chinese economy depends upon its ability to meet the essential requirements of the people. Improved agriculture and the retention of a larger share of the produce by the peasant has created an increased demand for manufactured goods. These demands must be met either by domestic production or by imports. Mr. Chen

Yun, whom I have quoted above, estimates the industrial potential in his 1950 report. "The few modern industries we have, constituting only 10 per cent of our national economy, are in a very weak and unstable condition."

China, like India, is an underdeveloped country. A large percentage of her few modern industries were formerly owned and managed by the foreign industrialists who had settled in Shanghai, Tientsin, Canton and Manchuria. With their eviction by the new government, China is faced with the problem of finding the technical skill and managerial ability to maintain even her limited production.

It is often forgotten that the reintegration of Manchuria into China has been a vital gain to the Chinese industry. During the occupation years Japan had tripled her investments in Manchuria. These investments covered many spheres of economic activity and developed the natural resources of the country. Coal, iron and steel, copper, zinc, gold and oil provided the nucleus for a considerable industrial development for which power was supplied from the hydroelectric project across the Korean border on the Yalu River. The machine tool industry at Anshan and Mukden, textile production and the manufacture of small electrical equipment were also enlarged. Manchuria's economic wealth is vital to the industrial future of China. For pointing this out in the thirties, the Nankai University at Tientsin was bombed out of existence by the Japanese.

I was therefore glad of the opportunity to visit Manchuria. At the end of the war news agencies in India had given long accounts of the Russian occupation of the area, and how they had stripped the industrial plants of all their machinery. In Peking I had learned that it was the Kuomintang reactionaries and not the Russians who had been the vandals. "Russians took some machinery but they returned it all," one high dignitary told me. Another had told me that "most" of the machinery had been returned by the Russians. Each successive question revealed the gradations of truth under communism. It was a long and irksome task to uncover facts. I learned from one of the few technical experts China has that many of the industrial plants were denuded by the Russians who, in fact, had returned nothing, and that the vandalism of the Kuomintang troops only added to the sorry plight in which the plants are found today.

The railroad journey across the country offered prospects of learning more about China. Peking was Mao Tsetung, Chou En-lai and a score of other Party bosses. China had been a continent lacking the modern apparatus of a state and united only by the traditional code of living. A dictatorship, on the other hand, needs a vast, unified and all-pervasive administration. The strength of Peking depended upon what machine it had been able to set up in the short time it had had.

The visit to the industrial Northeast commenced with the Industrial and Agricultural Exhibition in Mukden. The exhibition was concerned with only products of the Northeast, and a wide range of industrial equipment and consumer goods was shown. All kinds of steel, machine tools including precision lathes, turbines, generators and electric motors, cables, light and heavy chemicals, synthetic gasoline and gasoline products, glassware, pottery and textiles were to be seen. In many cases small models of the industrial plants showing various processes were shown. The exhibition was technically perfect and was organized with meticulous care to educate the visitor and make him industrially minded. At every stall there were young boys and girls to reel off an explanation of the exhibits, though they hardly seemed to understand what they said. Busloads of people were brought from the outlying districts to see the exhibition and they went away much impressed. So were many of the Asian visitors, for they had never been inside an ordinary modern factory. They had little idea of technical skill and the number of experienced craftsmen needed to carry out even simple operations. If they knew they would have realized that none of the wonderful machines exhibited could possibly have been produced in China. This exhibition was no different from other Communist propaganda: perfect in detail, thorough in its execution and shrewd in its understanding of the human weakness to believe what it cannot comprehend.

Our program included visits to a lead- and copper-smelting plant and to another factory manufacturing mining machinery and locomotive wheels. These factories were managed by Party members whose old loyalty cards since the days of Yenan entitled them to the benefits of power. There were no experts or technicians on the staff. For all such guidance they referred their problems to the various bureaus at Mukden which were manned by Russian experts. When such reference was made, the Soviet experts visited the plant and gave the necessary advice and guidance. The interesting fact was that when a worker was elected a "model worker" he was classified simultaneously as a "technician." These "technicians" were present when visitors came to the plant. They received higher wages and many other privileges, and their status is an incentive to the other workers. In one of the plants, it was admitted that all the skilled workers during the Japanese occupation had been Japanese—but now they had overcome the need for skill by the adoption of safety measures and health protection schemes!

It was evident that much of the work was carried out by manual labor. Large parts of the mining machinery plant with its big workshops were empty shells. In one spacious workshop there was only a broken overhead crane; in another a few workers were learning how to hammer a square rod of iron with the help of a pneumatic hammer; in a third locomotive wheels were being cast by hand. Only in one workshop were there some lathes, cutters and planers. The only purpose of this once productive plant's feeble endeavors seemed to be to employ workers and train them gradually in factory procedures for the day when equipment would become available. Cost in Communist economy is of no consequence. It is the value it gives to propaganda which matters. I had learned at the exhibition that China produced mining machinery; I was in the plant which claimed to manufacture it—but there was not one finished machine anywhere. I asked to be shown a unit in the process of assembly. I was told that as soon as a machine was ready it was immediately dispatched, for "our needs are so urgent." The lead- and copper-smelting plant was in a slightly better condition. But much of its work was carried on by manual labor and there was neither planning nor expert guidance.

It was difficult to see why we were being taken through these plants unless it was to impress upon us that China was carrying on against all difficulties. I was impressed with the determination to overcome all odds, but I wondered if these difficulties would not have been easier to overcome had there been a more realistic approach to international understanding. Or was it that circumstances had left no alternative but to rely on Soviet Russia for the means to improve the conditions of the Chinese people? There is no doubt that Russia was fully exploiting the helpless position of China for her own benefit.

On my second visit to Mukden eight months later I was hoping to see some progress in industrial equipment and efficiency. Russia and Eastern Europe could, after all, supply many of the essential needs in capital goods. Besides Russia had given sixty million dollars per year, under the Sino-Soviet Agreement, as a loan at 1 per cent interest for five years to be used in "payment for deliveries from the U.S.S.R. of equipment and materials including equipment for electric power stations, metallurgical and engineering plants, mining equipment for extraction of coal and ores, railway and other transport equipment, rails and other materials for the restoration and development of the national economy of China." If the agreement had any real significance China must be receiving vital assistance for the reconstruction of her shattered industry. I did not, however, expect any large-scale aid, for I had heard in Peking from a reliable source that China was unable to get any equipment and the little she had been able to buy was from Eastern Europe on long-term deliveries.

I was therefore interested when the program at Mukden this second time included a visit to a locomotive factory and a machine tool plant. But, as on the previous occasion, the visit began with a day at the industrial exhibition and the locomotive factory was forgotten. When we repeated our wish to see something of the Manchurian industry, we were told that a visit to a coal mine was being arranged in place of the locomotive factory. We were also told that the factory actually did not build locomotives but repaired rail coaches and manufactured wheels. I remembered the plant I had seen on the previous visit and could understand the Chinese concern not to take the visitors there again.

The visit to the coal mine and the shale oil refinery proved interesting from more points of view than one. Before the Sino-Japanese War China used to export coal to Japan. Today there are no such exports and coal is an important item in any policy of price stabilization. If China could resume her coal production and bring it back to its prewar level, it would not only help exports but also provide necessary fuel for her industries. I had read in the June issue of *China Monthly Review* that the coal output of the Tatung Colliery was 284 per cent higher in 1951 than in 1950. I knew this meant little for I had watched the few mules carrying small chunks of coal on the road from the mines at Tatung. It seemed an excellent opportunity to see the great coal field at Fushun.

The drive to Fushun from Mukden lies along an undulating countryside dotted with smoke-belching chimneys of Japan's industrial enterprise in Manchuria. Fushun itself is, like Mukden, an entirely Westernized but Japanese city. Its broad avenues are gray with coal dust while the residential area has all the amenities, including a race course. We were taken to the famous Ling Fung mines, given cotton pads to wear over our mouths and marched to the pithead. We then watched an occasional truck coming up from the bottom bringing up coal. We could not see how the mines were being worked or estimate whether production had risen to four times the "before liberation" production, as was claimed. One had to accept the figure and be content to learn that ten thousand workers were employed and housed with many benefits. Many of the visitors had seen enough and returned to Mukden.

Later in the day, the few of us remaining at Fushun went to see the open coal pit. This was a magnificent sight. The pit is almost a small canyon, 7,000 yards long, 300 to 1,200 yards wide and 170 yards deep. The soft coal seams here were 80 to 90 meters deep. Above the coal there is shale. On the edge of the pit stands the shale oil refinery, a vital defense industry. Unlike any other plant which I visited in the Northeast, this refinery was working to its full capacity. Ninety per cent of the plant, according to the information supplied, had been reconstructed by the government of New China, and production restored to its pre-war level.

One more industrial plant, a machine tool factory manufacturing lathes and cutters, was on our schedule. They were simple machines and did not require a high degree of skill. Here for the first time I saw a few machines imported from Russia. Interestingly, the name plates on all but one of the precision machines had been changed into Chinese characters. It explained the "Chinese" origin of many of the things we had seen at the exhibition. When I asked where such precision machines were manufactured, I was told that the Anshan Machine Tools Company, which unfortunately was not on the schedule, made them. It was clearly apparent from this and other evidence that no precision machines are manufactured in China.

The case of the textile industry is somewhat different. British industrialists in Shanghai admitted that the Chinese had the necessary skill and managerial ability to carry it on efficiently. Most of the textile mills are situated inside the Great Wall and particularly at Shanghai. Many of them, like a number of other light industries, are in the hands of private capitalists. There are British interests also. But they are all under the control of the government organization called the China Cotton Yarn and Cloth Company. Under this control, the government supplies the cotton and takes the finished product, after paying certain processing charges. As the product is standardized, there is little chance for initiative or profit. I visited a textile mill owned and managed by a private industrialist in Tientsin and another run by the state in Shanghai.

Cloth is, second only to food, a vital necessity for the underclothed millions in China. Adequate supplies are essential for economic stability. It forms an important item in the Parity Deposit Unit by which public confidence is maintained in the national currency. The textile industry is therefore a most important factor in China's reconstruction plans. She claims today that she is self-sufficient in her cloth requirements and the peasant is buying more and more cloth than ever before. Food and cloth are cited as examples of the prosperity of her masses. Peng Chen, the Mayor of Peking, had claimed that the peasant who was buying only 10.8 feet of cloth per person in 1949 was buying 24 feet of cloth in 1951 * as a result of his increased purchasing power resulting from land reform.

In a village home in Kao Kang in the Northeast, the peasant had proudly told his visitors that before the "liberation" he had only one patched and torn suit of clothes. Today he had five new suits! It was a visible sign of the economic and psychological satisfaction of the teeming population of China.

But China had been short of cotton and cloth in the past.

* The current official figure is 16 yards per person.

She had imported large quantities of cloth from Japan. India used to export cotton for Chinese industry. China has no more than five million spindles and in 1951 many of the textile mills had suspended manufacture for six weeks because of the shortage of cotton. If all the spindles had worked all the year round, I knew, they could not manufacture more than 2,000 million yards of cloth; and there were no longer any imports because of the blockade. It is therefore clear that despite all the improvements in efficiency claimed to have been attained by the Chinese textile workers, the country cannot produce enough cloth to meet the essential needs of her people. Production within China, her only source of supply, has led to standardization of cloth, high prices and scarcity. A yard of ordinary cloth costs about forty-two cents.

I had seen the young officials who looked after us wear day after day the same blue suit, unwashed and unironed, for they were given a single cotton suit a year! How then was China meeting her cloth requirements?

Pien Shih-ching, managing director of Hengyuan textile mill at Tientsin, is a model private capitalist owner of a model industrial enterprise. When he received me in October, 1951, he had already achieved the distinction of being a progressive capitalist who had sensed long before others what the wise course of action was to be. He was impressive looking despite a bald head. His bespectacled face bore the usual scraggy and drooping mustache of the mandarin. Unlike other national capitalists, he was dressed surprisingly in a blue Sun Yat-sen uniform, but it was clean and very well tailored. His firm but delicate hands and quiet manners indicated that he knew well how to handle his working-class masters. He offered us perhaps the best tea we ever had in China as he told us of his course of action. In 1950 he had experienced a shortage of cotton and the difficulties of obtaining supplies as a private individual. He therefore went to the government C.C.Y.C.C. (China Cotton Yarn and Cloth Company) and offered to enter into a two-year contract to deliver to them all the cloth he manufactured if the government supplied him with cotton and paid him only the processing charges. The government accepted the offer and took over the liability of the commodity tax on yarn and cloth which comes to about 17 per cent of the value of the cloth. The arrangements worked satisfactorily for Mr. Shih-ching, for the company paid a 7½ per cent dividend to its shareholders and retained about 10 billion yuans ($448,000) as undivided profits. As a model industrialist Mr. Shih-ching also enjoyed ideal labor relations.

As usual the trade union leaders and model workers were all present when we arrived at the Hengyuan Mill. But we received no report couched in official terms of how the industry was being worked. Mr. Shih-ching wanted no speeches and much preferred to answer our questions. He knew his work well and was quite content to take us around, answering our requests for specific information as we moved along. It was a change from other visits and when I asked for production details, he did not evade the answer. It was quite evident that he had managed to keep his working-class masters quite pleased.

When I returned to Tientsin on my second visit the Anti-Five campaign, a purge of government and industry, was in its last stages. I was anxious to see Mr. Shih-ching again but the request to visit the Hengyuan mill went unheeded. Perhaps the model industrialist had disappeared in the holocaust.

The pattern of the contract worked out by the Tientsin textile mill was an exception to the general practice. The processing charges paid to the mills in Shanghai left little profit for the industrialists. The British industrialists told me that due to commodity, business and stamp taxes they had hardly any surplus funds left, though the C.C.Y.C.C. which took over the finished cloth was making large profits from the sales. It was generally admitted, however, that of all enterprises, only the textile industry had any prospects of success in the present-day setup. It was able to work most of the year and could at least make ends meet.

I also visited a fertilizer plant near Nanking managed by Dr. Howe, a world-renowned technical expert. He lived for many years in the United States and is today the technical director of the Yung-ling Chemicals as well as adviser to the government. There are plans for the expansion of the chemical industry and while I was in Nanking the manager of the plant left for Eastern Europe to obtain machinery.

In Shanghai I talked to many other industrialists, mostly foreign. My impression that many plants had to remain idle three weeks out of each month because raw materials were short or because there was little demand was confirmed. The big tobacco plant of the Imperial Tobacco Company worked at one-third capacity though the Chinese are known to be heavy smokers. There were barrels of beer lying unsold at EWO Breweries, and many Chinese prefer to drink beer rather than rice wine.

It seems fair to conclude, therefore, that during the last three years China's attempts to revive and restore her industry are marked by effort rather than accomplishment. Shortages of capital goods and raw materials have prevented any sizable growth. In many cases she has been compelled to resort to handicraft production to meet her most immediate and pressing needs. Meanwhile, by austerity living and extremely high prices for outdated goods, she has held in check all demands.

In a shop in Nanking I saw imported English bicycles for $225 and Japanese-made cycles priced from $98 to $170. Bicycles were the only means of transport in the big cities apart from tramcars and dilapidated pedicabs.

China is utilizing to the maximum the little equipment she has to train her workers and make the people machine-minded. I saw this vividly at yet another industrial exhibition in Tientsin, which was a fine example of how to educate the people into feeling that their country was accomplishing what had never been attempted before. By a series of simple posters every activity of the people was directed into the set purposes of the state. Agriculture, industry, education, health, art and culture all were illustrated to show the aims and achievements of New China. Among the exhibits was a motorcar which the Communist zeal of the Chinese workers had helped to manufacture! Here was a solid achievement of the workers' state attained without equipment or knowhow! Whether that car would ever be able to travel along the road is something else again, but it did have under its hood an internal combustion engine.

It is not enough to publish figures of percentage increases. Occasionally the people must be shown a life-size model—even, if necessary, to put it in an exhibition with a live engine in it. Then the people can believe what was before only imaginary to them. In such ways does propaganda become convincing. I saw its effect among some of my colleagues who came back and told India that China manufactures motorcars, synthetic petrol and other things which a poor Asian imagines will be within his reach someday.

7

INFLATION AND FINANCE

At the end of the war, the Chinese economy found itself in complete ruin. Many of its industries were shattered and machinery removed, as in Manchuria. Railways were at a standstill and the rolling stock was in poor condition. Agriculture was disorganized and wide areas suffered from famines while farmers hoarded food grains. The financial disorder added to the distress of the people, who did not know from day to day the value of money they held. Prices changed hourly, leaving little alternative but to convert whatever money one had into goods. People had no confidence in the currency, so trade was almost paralyzed. It is estimated that in 1949 the local currency controlled only one-fortieth of the trade, while gold and foreign currencies became the only means of exchange. Meanwhile the Kuomintang continued printing currency notes until prices bore little relation to the money in circulation and depended instead upon the confidence—or, rather, the lack of it—of the people. In 1949, the currency in circulation was 176.8 billion times the currency in circulation before the war and the price index was 13,884.2

billion times. This meant that if a person had 10,000 Chinese dollars before the war, in 1949 he could not buy a matchstick with the money.

The state of affairs had so affected production that it was reduced by more than 30 per cent in agriculture and by 50 per cent in industry. No state could continue in this chaos. It is to the credit of the Communist regime that it effectively handled the situation and brought back order and confidence into the economic life of the people within a short period. Much of the present popularity of the government among the small traders and the business and industrial community is based on this return to security. Today, prices are fairly stable and, though the tendency toward inflation persists due to economic unbalance, the people feel confident and secure.

The process of deflation was carried out in three months —March-June, 1950—and the clogged channels of economic life were restored to make the transition from wartime to peacetime economic reconstruction possible. Perhaps such quick results are obtainable only in a totalitarian economy, but the effectiveness with which they were carried out shows the administrative capacity of the new regime. Three things were necessary to restore the currency to its normal function. First, the budget revenues and expenditures had to be brought under control and balanced. Secondly, the people had to be assured that the money in their possession would retain its exchange value; and finally prices had to be controlled so as to maintain this confidence.

To achieve the first aim, the state finances were put in order. All revenue was centralized and its expenditure was thereafter controlled by the government. Peasants were asked to pay their land tax in food grains and cotton. Industry was ordered to keep on working and the government took over its produce. Railroads were also reopened under a determined policy that "where the troops go the railroad goes." All these reforms led to a great increase in the state revenues. On the other hand spending was drastically controlled. Many government employees receive no pay. They work on a supply basis, and are given lodging, board, minimum rations and clothing. Military expenditures were kept separate and, it is claimed, the army put on a self-supporting basis. Nan Han-chen, the Chairman of the People's Bank, claimed that by these measures the deficit was reduced to such an extent that 100 million dollars in bonds issued that year covered all the country's needs. These bonds were issued at a fixed value in terms of commodities or silver dollars.

The second end, a stable exchange value, was realized by the creation of a "Parity Deposit Unit." Government organizations and enterprises, schools and the armed forces were ordered not to keep more money in cash on hand than what they needed for their expenses for three days. People were asked to deposit their surplus funds in the banks on an understanding that the money so deposited would be calculated in terms of units, the value of which would be guaranteed to them whatever the current prices. The P.D.U. so calculated included rice, cloth, oil and household coal. Circulation of gold was declared illegal and people were asked to surrender it to the banks, which bought it at an arbitrarily low price. Foreign currencies were similarly withdrawn, and paid for at a rate of exchange which bore no relation to actual prices. The last two sources provided the state with moneys to pay for its imports. China's eight hundred private banks were put under the administrative authority of the People's Bank to prevent speculation in currency and trade.

Finally, prices were brought under control by putting the trade in food grains, cloth, coal and other necessities under a central authority. The government itself accumulated stocks of goods and sold them at fixed prices through government shops. Food was the main problem because other necessities which were hitherto hoarded emerged with the return of confidence. The government, however, received large quantities of food grains in the form of land tax. These receipts were enough to feed forty-five million people for the whole year, while the demand in the urban and famine area that year required food grains enough to feed about sixty million people. The government therefore bought additional food grains on the open market, and also collected taxes for 1949 as well as for 1950 in the course of the year. There was sufficient coal because there were no exports and what was mined, it is claimed, was adequate to meet the demands of the country.

It was Nan Han-chen who was called upon to explain China's fight against inflation to the many visitors who had come to Peking in October, 1951. As managing director of the People's Bank he controlled the financial and monetary policies of China. I was told he had been once a clerk in the Bank of China under the Kuomintang regime. Today, he faithfully and brilliantly carries out the difficult policy which has helped to maintain some equilibrium in spite of enormous economic difficulties. He is the master mind behind the policy of flooding the country with currency and then squeezing it back so as to maintain some stability in prices. He spoke to the visitors for almost three hours on a subject which was perhaps dry and uninteresting to many, but he held their attention by the simplicity of his exposition, and his quiet mannerisms fascinated many of them. I do not think he is a member of the Communist Party, but like Dr. Schacht, he is loyal to his regime and, as an expert, is willing to carry out her policies.

He described the success of his policy: "We have now no hoarding, no scarcity of commodities. By preventing the dumping upon us, or the import, of food grains and cloth which we do not need, we have given an impetus to industrial and agricultural production in our own country by widening the markets for them. Hence trade has increased and along with it the notes in circulation also have increased. We have balanced our budget. We have enough foreign exchange. For the last year and more, we have maintained financial and price stability. Sometimes there may have been isolated cases of short supply, but we have tried to remedy them. We have reorganized and restored the productive capacities of our industries which are useful to the economy of the country, and serve the people. We have undertaken vast irrigation schemes like the Huai River project and reduced the area chronically affected by famines from twenty million acres to about seven million acres. We still have a certain disparity between agricultural and industrial prices which we cannot eliminate in such a short period but we shall overcome it by rapid industrialization."

This was indeed an impressive record narrated to the visitors in October, 1951. The basic need had been to gain the faith of the people in the national currency and prohibit the use of foreign currencies and gold as a means of exchange. The institution of the Parity Deposit Unit linked the currency to four essential commodities which were kept under absolute control. The government's willingness to accept the payment of land tax in kind and the fixing of wages in terms of rice or millet or kaoliang assured the peasantry and the workers of a stable standard of living, even though this standard was low. Any improvement in it depended upon increased production and not on income. The prices of other commodities rested on the availability of these commodities and the surplus money in the hands of the people.

Political stability was one of the important factors in gaining the confidence of the people. Inflation had continued despite attempts to check it. But when Mao returned from Moscow with Sino-Soviet alliance in February, 1950, it had an immediate effect on the currency. The New Democracy was henceforth firmly in saddle and only a world war could endanger its future. Gold and foreign currencies which had been hoarded were now surrendered to the People's Bank at low prices and the government was able to carry out its financial policy.

But the halt in prices proved only temporary. China like other dictatorships lives by printing currency. To maintain a huge army of five million, to finance long-term projects out of revenues and to keep the vast machinery of administration which a totalitarian regime involves are too great a burden on the limited resources of an underdeveloped country. Though actual figures of the budget * are not

* Toward the end of February, 1953, the Peking government announced for the first time the actual figures of the national budget. Finance Minister Po Yi-po said the national revenue amounted to about eight billion dollars in 1952 and expenditures during the year had left a net surplus of one billion dollars. Actually these figures have little meaning in terms of U.S. currency, since the foreign exchange is fixed arbitrarily and has no relation to the price index or the balance of trade. Nan Han-chen had told me, in reply to a question, that China's current

available, there can be no doubt that the revenues are insufficient for all the demands made on them. There is other evidence available to indicate that more currency is being put into circulation. There was an unmistakable rise in prices during 1950-51 and though the Chinese government admits a rise of only 13 per cent in agricultural prices and 19 per cent in industrial commodities, the actual rise may be 40 per cent as stated by a high official, or as much as 100 per cent as private interests contend.

Because all wages and fixed salaries in China are in terms of rice or millet, though they are paid in cash on the basis of the price on the day of payment, the increase in prices only affects the consumption of other commodities and not of the particular food grains. The increase in prices of food grains indicates a lowering of the value of currency, as it does not seek to adjust the demand for food grains to the supply. There is, however, no surplus purchasing power.

People's China, in trying to explain away this fact, writes rather naïvely:

The prices of some industrial commodities were bound to rise slightly, owing to the fact that the purchasing power of the masses and particularly of the peasants has been increasing steadily while the output of industrial goods has not yet caught up with the people's needs. Such a phenomenon is only a natural process of economic reconstruction. The 13.8 per cent

price index is twenty-five thousand times that of 1937. Apart from this, the essential difference between the budget figures of the Kuomintang regime and the present figures must be sought in the fact that large sections of industry have been nationalized and the state has a monopoly of foreign trade as well as a major part of the internal trade. Po Yi-po admitted that less than 50 per cent of the budget figures were revenues from taxes. The remainder was proceeds of the state-owned enterprises plus the exactions of the Anti-Three and Anti-Five campaigns. 16.51 per cent of the 1953 receipts is from "last year's balance and 'other sources.' " "Other sources" quite probably imply deficit financing.

rise in commodity prices last year is, therefore, actually a reflection of the rising purchasing power of the people.

It may be contended that there has been an increase in the wages of the workers and that this represents increased purchasing power in their hands. But similar increases in production have also been claimed and consequently the increased demand should have been met from the available supplies without a rise in prices. It must therefore be the need in the budget for cash currency which depreciates the value of money. Such a phenomenon is natural to deficit financing.

I believe the national budget is not balanced and the huge military expenditure and the cost of national projects are all being met by the simple device of printing notes as long as the power of the state keeps rigid control over the life of the people. The currency is not based in value on commodities or any other factor other than what the state decrees.

Apart from the price adjustment, the state regulates the currency in the hands of the people by the periodic demands for contributions which are voluntary only in name. Within the last three years, China has witnessed three such campaigns. First came the One Hundred Million Dollar Bonds, then the Aid Korea Resist America Fund in conjunction with the Fighter Planes Fund, and finally, early in 1952, the San Fan Wu Fan. All these campaigns extorted large funds from the people which would have otherwise been thrown on the market. Thus they are economic necessities apart from their practical value.

I met Nan Han-chen again on my second visit. As usual I sent my questions to his office in advance, and after several days was called there one afternoon to hear his replies.

"Our main sources of revenue," he said, "are (1) commodity taxes, business turnover taxes, income taxes and sales taxes, (2) income from state-operated industry, and (3) land revenue. Land revenue is not the major source of revenue. We have balanced our budget, and we hope we will have a surplus this year. We have sufficient savings in the country. We finance our development projects from our revenues. Our finances are rigidly handled by the central government. The revenues are allocated to the provinces according to previously arranged plans. There is no inflation in the country and prices are determined by supply and demand in the open market. It is true we use large stocks of commodities held by the government to keep prices within certain limits both in the interest of the consumer and the producer. The disparity between agricultural and industrial production does not necessitate price control. Chinese currency is not linked to any commodity or to the commodities included in the P.D.U. In fact we have three times the commodities in stock to the currency in circulation."

My interview had lasted more than an hour, and was strictly limited to the written questions I had sent. Nan Han-chen was determined to deny that there was an inflation, or that the government printed currency to meet its requirements and withdraw any surplus purchasing power in the hands of the people by means of compulsory "contributions." The previous year he had told me there was strict control over prices, but now he denied it. Yet his statements in this interview proved that there was a definite price policy and that the government had succeeded in extracting nearly two-thirds of the national income in terms of production from the people. High prices and purchasing power in the hands of the people limited to a minimum subsistence level accomplished it. It was evident at the same time that currency bore little relation to the cost of living. Money was the power of the state and was printed to serve the purposes of the state. It had little value.

8

THE CHINESE ECONOMY

THE Chinese economy, according to Prime Minister Chou En-lai, is divided into five parts, socialist in nature, under the leadership of the state. The state's function is to "co-ordinate and regulate" them "in their spheres of operations, supply of raw materials, marketing, labor conditions, technical equipment, policies of public and general finance, etc."

The five sectors are individual scale economy which includes family farms and all handicrafts; private capitalist enterprise; state capitalist enterprise representing a combination of state and private capital; co-operative enterprise; and nationalized enterprise. The last sector includes the enterprises once owned by foreign capitalists such as the Japanese, who have been driven out. Thus about 80 per cent of heavy industry and 30 per cent of light industry have been nationalized.

The coexistence of private agriculture and industry is accepted as an interim state between feudal China and a purely socialist China. Mao had written in *New Democracy:* "The first stage is new democracy, the second is socialism. But the duration of the first stage will be rather long." In describing the political and economic nature of the New Democratic Revolution he wrote:

Economically, it strives to nationalize all large capital interests, and all large enterprises of the imperialists, traitors, and reactionaries, to divide up the large estates and to distribute them among the peasantry, at the same time helping the middle and small private industries, while making no attempt to abolish the economy of rich farmers. Consequently, while this new kind of democratic revolution clears the way for capitalism, yet in another sense it is also creating a precedent for socialism.

Communist China appears to the visitor as a country of mixed economy with vast sectors still under private ownership where handsome profit is permitted. It is said that the state allows 15 per cent profit to the private capitalist, and a dividend up to 8 per cent can be declared by the joint stock companies. Apart from this, the law requires 10 per cent of the profits to be put into reserves. Of the balance, 60 per cent may be given as a bonus to shareholders and 15 per cent utilized for the workers' welfare. The example of Hengyuan textile mills was given to me as a now profitable industry which before the liberation had suffered great losses and had no capital left.

On the other hand, the British industrialists in China assert that there are no profits for industry. Even the textile mills, which obtain good prices for cloth, are just able to break even, they contend, since the government only pays them processing charges and earns profits for itself. In cases where the government permits them to sell directly, traders buy small quantities and stocks accumulate. The private trader has lost his market and the trade has gone into the hands of the government or the co-operative shops. In every town that I visited, I saw the government department stores filled with people, while other shops were deserted. The prices in the shops are fixed, but the shopkeeper is willing to come and sell the same merchandise at the buyers' homes at much reduced prices.

The Hengyuan mills had decided to erect another textile mill in Sian out of its reserves. A building was put up and machinery was purchased but the management was unable to get any technicians or workers in Sian. If these were transported from the industrial coastal region their wages would be much higher. Mr. Pien Shih-ching therefore went to the Economic and Finance Commission and explained his difficulties. The Commission then decided to take over the Sian plant.

This was a direct result of land reform. The peasant was unwilling to give up his land and become a wage laborer. It was otherwise in the coastal area where the per capita holding of land was only 1.7 mows, and there was, instead, a constant danger of unemployment.

Meanwhile government trading has expanded rapidly. An overwhelming proportion of imports and exports is handled by the state. From 40 to 100 per cent of the wholesale trade in food grains, coal, cotton goods, salt, sugar, iron, steel, timber and cement is in the hands of the government trading companies. Some 30 per cent of retail trade is also in the hands of the state and the co-operatives. Most of the large factories have signed long-term contracts to sell their entire output to the state.

The Chinese economy is not a mixed economy but an economy in which the state regulates and controls the private enterprises at key points so as to make them subservient to the purposes of the state. By allocation of output and raw materials, controls on cash and credit holdings, industrial and trade taxes and regulated distribution of profits, private enterprise is reduced to a mere feeder or contractor to state enterprise. Bulk purchases and state-run retail trade have given the government "price leadership" which enables it to dictate prices.

So the sphere of private trade has shrunk. Article 31 of the Common Program had prescribed this development: "Whenever necessary and possible, private capital shall be encouraged to develop in the direction of state capitalism in such ways as processing for state-owned enterprises and exploiting state-owned resources in the form of concession."

A major blow at the existence of private businessmen was struck by the San Fan Wu Fan movements when heavy fines were imposed on their meager savings. With few credit facilities and no business prospects, they are turning to smaller trades. All over China this shift is visible in the government figures of "expanding" private enterprise. Mao Tse-tung calls the national bourgeoisie the remaining reactionary class which "when the time comes to realize socialism" will be educated and reformed with the help of the people's army, police and courts. Obviously the logic of communism has led Mao to the necessity of liquidating the bourgeoisie within two years of "liberation." Mao's economic policy is in the process of transformation.

To improve the standard of living of her people, China has announced a five-year plan, under which, it is said, heavy industries will be developed and agriculture mechanized. But what little I saw in the country seems sufficient evidence that she has neither the technical resources nor the capital savings for its realization without considerable foreign assistance. China's problem requires that she maintain the people's living standards, which are now in a majority of cases on a below-subsistence level, while simultaneously providing employment, capital, knowhow and, above all, a willingness on the people's part to bear further heavy sacrifices. Though a dictatorship is capable of imposing heavy burdens on the people, it must still assure them some benefits in their daily life and a reasonable improvement in their standard of living. Thus they hear fulsome announcements of miraculous achievements; and it has been necessary to create an enemy to divert their attention from hardships within. Only a free people, freely prepared to bear the sacrifices of the present, can build for the future with true co-operation.

In the underdeveloped countries of Asia the state has not been able to compel its people to suffer further privations merely in the hope of a better future. Unless these countries are willing to pool their resources in order to minimize the sufferings of their people, and co-operate willingly with each other in peace and friendship, there can be no development or economic betterment of the masses. Asian countries urgently need foreign assistance, for they have little savings or equipment.

Communist China, however, has chosen to tread another path. For the time being, the dictatorship can finance the vast administration, the large standing army and partially reconstruct the shattered economy by imposing the burdens of deficit financing, and taxing the capacities of its people to the limit. But cheap conscript labor can build only earthworks on the Huai. It cannot relieve the pressure of population on the land, solve the problem of a peasantry fearfully guarding its small holdings or provide for employment and industrial development.

China is skillfully using the weapon of propaganda to counter the growing suspicions of the peasantry. America is the new enemy and the hatreds of a gentle people are being fanned to divert their attention. But the war in Korea is beginning to weary them. A new diversionary campaign against individualism, against the "reactionary" individual who wants peace and happiness or the peasant who seeks to retain his land is a very possible development. But there is a limit to the human capacity to suffer. Will the Chinese rise to reassert their freedom, or will their so-called "democratic dictatorship" lead them to adventure in other lands of Southeast Asia to make them forget their frustrated hopes? I believe it possible that Communist China will ultimately try to win to her side as allies the ten million Chinese residents in Southeast Asia.

Part Three

THE GREAT PEACE

1

BRAINWASHING

COMMUNISM relies on absolute acceptance of the faith and a mind which does not question. Brainwashing is thus an important part of its policy of thought control, or forcing all doubts, all sources of knowledge and the individual's right to think into one mold which claims to contain the final, absolute truth. It is therefore to be expected that Communist China will seek to control all education. The Common Program * ordains, "In order to meet the extensive requirements of revolutionary and national construction work, universal education shall be carried out," and education becomes but a means of serving the purposes of the new revolution.

The task is immense and involves changing the traditional characteristics of the Chinese people. For centuries China had developed a philosophy of living which rejected intolerance and harshness. It was an individualism tempered with knowledge that accepted the diversity of life. The Chinese scholar was the embodiment of earnest study, gentle living and a deep understanding of his fellow men.

* See Appendix.

There was no dogma and over the centuries even the disciplined and ascetic face of Buddha changed its serene beatitude into a smile both gentle and humane. New China is dogmatic, harsh and cruel.

I saw this cruelty in the nursery school at Shanghai run by Mme. Sun Yat-sen. There were more than two hundred children between the ages of three to seven. The Indian Delegation had been specially asked to the nursery, for Mme. Sun now devotes her whole energy to social work. The children put on a show for the guests. In the show, they marched as the People's Liberation Army, their toy guns pointed at the "American" planes above. They learned to hate and kill. In the classrooms they were being taught the five loves: love of the fatherland, love of the people, love of labor, love of science and care of public property. There was no love for parents or family, and these little children sorely missed it. They clung to the visitors and wanted to be fondled and kissed. Some had tears in their eyes as they were picked up and patted. I knew then what cruelty meant.

I saw it again and again elsewhere, in the clusters of small children that flocked around us, in the faces of men and women who wanted a little affection, a little humanity and friendship. There are no friendly faces in New China. Those who had lived for years in China spoke repeatedly of the Chinese smiling even in the midst of poverty. But now the faces are set and grim. A friend described the crying of the Chinese children under the New Democracy as shrieks of anger.

Mme. Sun's nursery held children who were learning the lessons of communism in their cradles. I wanted to see educational procedures on all levels, for China claimed to have established a national system of scientific and popular education which fostered the ideals of service by the people; so I went to the middle schools and the universities, to the workers' and peasants' middle schools and the People's University.

The Eighth middle school in Peking had nine hundred students. Among the sons of workers and peasants was the son of Vice-Premier Kuo Mo-jo. Old textbooks, curriculum and methods of teaching had been abolished, for the school served the "interests of the people" and followed the Soviet system. All the boys were members of the Youth League or the Young Pioneers and engaged in political activities. In one of the classes, a colleague accompanying us decided to ask a question: "What would you do if Soviet Russia attacked China?" "It shall never happen," the boy answered. "And who was Confucius?" "He was an outworn, feudal philosopher," said the boy.

The six-year course of the normal middle school was shortened to three years at the middle school for the workers and peasants. In China there are forty such schools with fifteen thousand workers and peasants who had helped in the revolution enrolled. Their education prepared them to become future village administrators as well as Party disciplinarians. Apart from learning how to read and write, they were taught Marxism, physics, chemistry and the history of the revolution. They lived in dormitories and were expected to keep watch on each other's thoughts. After they learned to write about one thousand words, they were made to keep daily diaries which must record all they felt and thought. These diaries were scrutinized in group discussion and the wrong ideas were "purged." So began the brainwashing.

THE GREAT PEACE

In an address to the People's Political Consultative Council on October 23, 1951, Mao had said, "The remolding of ideology, primarily the ideological remolding of the various types of intellectuals, is an important condition for the thorough carrying out of democratic reforms." This nation-wide process was carried on in five stages. The first stage was criticism and self-criticism. Chou En-lai began the movement with himself. The second stage was to learn to distinguish between enemies and friends, to draw a clear line of demarcation around reactionary ideas and to establish absolute rejection of such ideas. This stage was inaugurated by Peng Chen, the Mayor of Peking, who spoke about land reform, Kuomintang agents and American "imperialism." In the third and fourth stages Mao Tse-tung's thoughts on communism and Chinese economic structure were imparted. Finally each individual was called upon to report on his personal conclusions and thus undergo further examination.

During this process, professors, writers and other intellectuals underwent a reorientation of thought. I met a professor of economics who was trying to forget all the education he had received at Oxford University. Dr. Fong and Dr. Ling, famous professors of philosophy at Tsinhua University, had learned that old Chinese philosophy was a worn-out feudal concept. They publicly recanted all that they had written and had begun to learn anew the philosophy of Communist materialism.

Kuo Mo-jo, the Vice-Premier of China, poet and famous archeologist, said in answer to my question about intellectual freedom in China, "The writer in China has freedom to express himself as long as he serves the interest of the workers, peasants and soldiers who are the majority of the people."

Brainwashing continued at maximum efficiency in the People's University. The president of the university, Wu Yu-chang, is a member of the Executive Committee of the Communist Party. The university was established in 1950. Out of 2,800 students, 2,000 were cadres whose cultural level was "low" and had been sent to the university for a one-year course to improve their standard. Culture in China implies Marxism and the cadres were here because their "historical viewpoint" had been found wanting in loyalty to the ideology. Of the two thousand students 71.7 per cent had three to seven years of government experience, which implied that many were Kuomintang officials who were continued in office or those whose education was not completed during the war. Of the remaining, 22 per cent were intelligentsia and the rest were workers.

The short course included theoretical study and "productive" work. Economics, finance, banking, trade, co-operation, factory management and diplomacy were taught, but 70 per cent of their time was occupied in "practice in production." The full-course students learned the same subjects, plus economic planning, law and Russian. There was in addition a special section in the university called Teaching Research groups. There were thirty-seven such groups, whose function is to check the effectiveness of the teaching program, study teaching methods, Marxism and Maoism, and keep an eye on the staff. These groups are in fact the "cells" which maintain a close hold on the life of the students and the staff.

As usual, when we visited the university, there were hardly any students in sight except the few selected ones who were introduced to us as models. We met a seventeen-year-old peasant student who had been in the People's Liberation Army and had been captured by the Japanese. Another student was a coal miner's son. He was a member of the executive committee of his trade union. He had been a labor model and was now a member of the People's Political Consultative Committee. We were then shown an exhibition of the students' work which included the well-known diaries. One can easily imagine the terror which the students must feel when their diaries have to be produced and discussed in the classroom. There were also the usual dormitories where the students lived in close proximity and under one another's observation.

Mr. Wu, the president, admitted that there was a shortage of teachers, teaching materials, textbooks and equipment. The students relied on notes they took in class since all the old textbooks had been discarded. Some of the professors and teachers who had been trained in Russia had prepared teaching notes and these notes were circulated to all the universities in the country. The professors and teachers had undergone a "reorientation of thought" and it was tragic to see these men educated in many parts of the world trying to forget the knowledge they had acquired. Academic qualifications counted for little and men with Party cards directed education. The head of the famous Medical College in Mukden was a thirty-five-year-old "comrade" who had not even completed his education. He had learned medicine "under the supervision of foreign friends during the War of Liberation."

I visited the Tsinghua, Yenching and the Peking National Universities at Peking, the Nankai at Tientsin and the Nanking University at Nanking. China is concentrating

on her youth for she needs them to man the ever-growing
administration of the country and provide the scientific and
technical skill for her development. These universities had
once been centers of liberal and progressive thought and
had cradled the May Fourth movement against imperialism.
Today the spirit of youth marches in procession from
morning till late evening to the beat of the drum and the
clang of cymbals preaching hatred of the Americans and
loyalty to totalitarian New China.

During the San Fan Wu Fan and the Aid Korea and Resist America movements the students, with their Youth
League leaders or the Young Pioneers, were inculcated
with the theory and practice of the New Democracy. Four
months the colleges and universities were closed while the
students and professors participated in protracted sessions,
each criticizing the deficiencies of others and sometimes
confessing to their own. In one instance one of the foreign
professors was reprimanded by the students for choosing
reactionary subjects for their essays. They would have,
they insisted, much rather written their essays on germ
warfare.

Miss Wu was a professor at a woman's college in Nanking. She was charming, intelligent and a popular teacher.
A colleague had a letter of introduction to her, and when
we were in Nanking tried to see her. She had been compelled to leave the college, we were told, and had gone to
Shanghai—perhaps because she had not submitted to the
brainwashing. When we tried to see her in Shanghai a
frightened, bewildered woman spoke to us on the tele-
phone and cut the conversation short. A few days later I
learned she had committed suicide.

A well-known professor of biology also appears to have

met the same fate. His crime was to teach in more than one college and be paid for it. On April 19, 1952, the daily newspaper, *Yi-po* of Tientsin, reported him as a "swindler." It asked, "What could such a professor do besides delaying our youth? All righteous people and all those resolved to serve the people must be earnest in undergoing ideological remolding and in opposing all rotten bourgeois ideology."

In the colleges and schools, life begins with Marxism and ends with Maoism. There was nothing before except "all dogma and false philosophies." All over the country, in government offices and in important jobs, I found youth in charge. Hardly had they finished their studies than they enlisted in the service of the state. It mattered little whether the individual wanted to be an engineer or a doctor or a professor. China needed the services of all those who could be called educated. Education is a privilege only a few could attain; there are today 135,000 students in all the universities of China. It is hoped that next year there will be room for 150,000.

Education is free in both schools and colleges—as it was even in the Kuomintang days. Those who have the privilege of going to the universities are distributed throughout the country by a Central Co-ordinating Authority. Standards of education are low. Scientific or technical education is further limited by the need of solving day-to-day problems of agriculture or industry, at the expense of basic research and abstract study. Well-known scientists are occupied with experiments such as the manufacture of DDT from the local raw materials. Famous scholars are trying to evolve scientific terms in Chinese.

Yet I heard claims of research in atomic science in Sinkiang. Rumor had it that the British atomic scientist, Dr.

Bruno Pontecorvo, who fled the West while on a vacation in Italy, is now working there. The Natural Resources Exhibition in Canton had a uranium rock on exhibit. This talk of research and inventions, however, of education and scientific knowledge, has little meaning for there is no real education. It is rather the indoctrination and subordination of youth to the greater glory of communism.

One of our woman interpreters had been educated at Columbia University in New York. It took us many days to learn that she had been abroad to study. When we discovered this, we asked, "How did you enjoy your stay in America?" "I hated every minute of it," she replied. Her parents, we found, lived in Nanking. For more than a year she had not seen them and Mrs. Pandit, on our arrival there, suggested that she go and visit them. But she declined to leave Mrs. Pandit alone even when she promised she would not leave the hotel.

In the whole group of interpreters of young men and women from the Foreign Office and the Institute of Foreign Languages, who were attached to the Delegation, I never came across a smiling friendly face. Only one evidenced any warmth of feeling for us in spite of the fact that we had been together constantly for six weeks. He hovered around us the day of our departure, embraced us warmly and had tears in his eyes as he bade us good-by. I hope his sentiment was not noticed by the Chinese officials, for otherwise, I am afraid, he will have to go through another course of brainwashing.

Mr. Chang was our interpreter. He was a Shanghai graduate and spoke English and some French. He was unemotional, totally humorless, and seldom relaxed. On our last day in China, Canton was hot and full of mosquitoes. In the broken-down hotel in the old British Concession very few of us had been able to sleep at night. We had come down to breakfast tired and a little irritable except for one of our colleagues who was always full of fun. He turned to Chang and said, "I did not sleep a wink last night. The mosquitoes kept on sucking my blood. I shall call them landlords, Chang." Chang's ire was roused for there were no land-lords in China. He sharply replied, "No, not landlords, but American imperialist aggressors." We all laughed while Chang sat fuming and silent.

I met several selfless young men who had dedicated themselves to the service of their country. Many of them have returned from abroad and are today working on meager salaries, leading hard and austere lives. I know all religious faiths attract selfless devotion and Chinese com-munism is no exception. But there is none of that reckless, irresponsible élan which is the right of youth. There was no joy of love or sorrow of frustration; hope could express itself only in spying, informing and accusing, to show one's loyalty to the state and its ideology.

Only in one educational sphere has China made a signifi-cant attempt. Adult literacy was a big problem and the manner in which it has been handled shows progressive re-sults. The Chinese language was simplified and a knowl-edge of eight hundred to a thousand words enabled the people to read simplified newspapers and learn something about the country in which they lived. The People's Liberation Army had learned to read and write on its long marches. Now, in the cities and the villages, men and women were taught by students, shopkeepers and man-agers. Two hours daily were devoted to this task. And those who had learned showed off their knowledge to others with obvious pride.

The task of reorienting the minds of the people is a big one. Intolerance and dogmatism are alien to the whole tradition of China. Many scholars and professors have accepted the brainwashing and its accompanying terror because they feel that in spite of it all they can serve China. There is acceptance of regimentation and discipline. Few people in the world have such immense attachment to the land of their birth.

Life is earnest while youth prepares itself for the tasks of the nation. Young China was seriously applying itself to the study of theory and practice of communism. I have heard it said that the youth has now come into its own and as such is happy and determined. An English ecclesiastic in Shanghai said, "In my twenty-eight years' experience I have never seen a greater zest for learning than now. In their spare time the older students conduct literacy classes for workers while the younger teach primary classes." I have seen hundreds of these young men of China marching, with flags flying, to a Wu Fan meeting or to a Sunday picnic. I have seen determination and relentless pursuit of ambition. I have watched them working long hours writing daily diaries to be submitted to their superiors. But I have not seen happiness. The youth of China knows that the future belongs to it, but in that future it can only have a place if it becomes an automaton in a totalitarian-purposive state.

2

"REFORM THROUGH LABOR"

THERE have been serious charges of the liquidation of millions of people leveled against the Chinese Communist government in the democratic press. The civil war had taken a heavy toll of human life. Mao Tse-tung has himself admitted in his address to the Preparatory Committee Meeting of the Chinese People's Political Consultative Conference that in three years, the People's Liberation Army had wiped out 5,900,000 reactionary Kuomintang troops. He then said, "At the present time, the remnants of the Kuomintang Army, including regular and irregular forces, as well as rear area military organizations and military schools, number only about 1½ million men. It will still take a certain time to clean up these remaining troops but not too long." In September, 1951, Premier Chou En-lai said that these million and a half reactionaries had been "liquidated." It is a small wonder that charges of massacre should follow such admissions.

In October, 1951, I read in Peking that a People's Trial was going on in Canton in which 676 reactionaries were involved. In Tihua, at the same time, 234 people were being tried for the same crime. These trials received only small notices in the local press. I was therefore anxious to learn more about the great liquidation drive in the country. Very little information was available and I had to rely on gossip and rumor and then sift them as far as possible.

The Kuomintang troops left behind by Chiang had spread out all over the country and hidden their arms. China is well known for her secret societies and many of these agents joined such societies. They were further strengthened, especially in the South, by the landlords, who were facing extinction under the land reform. Soon after the proclamation of the Republic, the government of China decreed that all those who had been members of the Kuomintang troops should register themselves. If they did so, the government promised, they would be treated generously. Only those who refused to confess were rounded up. As the land reform progressed the landlords and their private armies resisted in many cases. In Shanghai, I was told, between three and five thousand people were picked up and shot.

Mao had stated in 1949 that the present task of the People's Government was to strengthen the People's Army, the People's Police and the People's Courts, because "such state apparatus as the army, the police and the courts are the instruments with which one class oppresses another." He denied that the People's Government had any intention of following a generous policy toward other classes. "We definitely have no benevolent policies toward the reactionaries or the counterrevolutionaries," he said in the same speech. "Our benevolent policy does not apply to such persons who are outside the rank of the people; it applies only to the people."

It is clear that the Chinese government intended to deal firmly with these groups who did not fall within the term "people" and ultimately eliminate them as a class. The method adopted was either death or "reform through labor." "As for those belonging to reactionary classes or groups," said Mao, "we will give them land and work and permit them to make a living and to reform themselves through labor into new persons. If they do not want to work, the People's State will force them to do so."

Liquidation, therefore, does not necessarily mean death. In the Chinese terminology it means "to render ineffective." In the Canton trials to which I referred above, 22 persons were sentenced to death, 11 were also sentenced to death but their sentences were suspended for a period of two years, 16 were released and the remaining 627 were sentenced to imprisonment which, in this case, could be in a concentration camp. In Tihua 18 were sentenced to death, 6 to death after two years, 11 were released and 199 were sentenced to various terms of imprisonment.

The procedure followed in these investigations was entirely in the hands of the Police Security Office. This office was in charge of collecting evidence, inviting confessions or accusations from the public and framing the charges against the accused. It also recommended the punishment. The case was then reviewed by a committee which decided upon the sentence. Finally, a public trial took place where the witnesses came forward with their accusations. At the trial, the accused could not defend himself because he was not allowed to speak. Only during the investigation could he contradict or deny the testimony, but there was no cross-examination nor a lawyer to look after his interests. The public trial is a form of propaganda machinery to inspire fear and obedience. The sentences of imprisonment led the accused to concentration camps which are euphemistically called "Reform through Labor Camps."

One day in late October, when I was in Nanking, there appeared a description of such a camp in the *Hsinhua Pao*, a well-known daily newspaper, under the heading "Ching Ha Farm for Counterrevolutionaries." The article was translated for me by the interpreter and makes interesting reading.

The Bureau of Public Security started Ching Ha Farm a year ago for reforming counterrevolutionaries; by now they have achieved success not only economically but also politically, because many criminals have already reformed their reactionary thoughts through participation in productive work. Many criminals show a great zeal in work, and thus repent for what they have done and turn over a new leaf. Ching Ha Farm was established in March, 1950; at that time the place was barren land, without any habitations. Now this farm has established 8 new villages, 2,500 rooms,* dug a canal 1,500,000 cubic feet, i.e. more than 20 li long; also they have built a power station so that they can pump water and irrigate more than 50,000 mows of land and supply electricity. They now have telephones, a hospital, engineering team, transportation team, laboratory, machinery group, brick kilns, rice flour mill, and also manufacture straw bags.

When these criminals first came to the farm, most of them were not used to doing any work and did not know production technique. Most of them even feared and hated the very idea of working. Many of them were indirectly on strike; when carrying earth, for example, they would pretend to fall

---

* This implies that there were more than 10,000 prisoners on the farm. Generally, the Chinese workers' homes house fourteen to sixteen persons a room. A room 10′ x 8′ would have a k'ang 8′ x 6′ for four persons to sleep.

down and thus take a rest, or they took a long time in the washroom and thus avoided work. Some of them openly refused to work and tried to sabotage the work by damaging instruments and helping criminals to escape. But through participation in work and through thought-education, a sharp change took place in the criminals' minds. Most of them now admit their crimes and want to reform themselves. Even when their term of sentence is over, some of them do not want to leave and would rather live and work on the farm.

How has this transformation been achieved on this farm? By following the principle that political reform must be accompanied by labor reformation. It was a difficult struggle to change their minds and a lot of work was necessary for thought-education. When Chairman Mao's "People's Democratic Dictatorship" was first explained to them and they were told about the plan for their reformation through labor, they showed great resistance against the idea—many cried, many went on hunger strikes, many wrote their last letters, and some even tried to commit suicide and to escape.

The cadres on the farm explained to the criminals that only by reformation through labor could they hope to have a new life. Also they gave them lessons in the development of society, and explained to them how labor has created the world and all in it. Thus they corrected the wrong attitude of the criminals toward labor which so far was one of hatred and contempt. But even after they started participating in labor, their thoughts were not immediately reformed and "stabilized," and were often influenced by outside situation—e.g. when American imperialists landed in Korea and the Korean People's Army retreated temporarily, many of the criminals were talking among themselves, expecting American victory and the return of Chiang Kai-shek.

After describing the steps taken for thought reform by political education, the article continues:

Still counterrevolutionaries cannot be reformed so easily, and a few of them are still unreformed and try to sabotage production and discipline of the farm. To such people the contrast between punishment and reward has to be sharply indicated. Both the methods of punishment and education have to be used in their case. On the other hand, in the case of criminals who genuinely repent their past crimes and show willingness to reform, their terms of sentences are shortened.

Thus from March, 1950, up to now, they have already freed more than two hundred of these reformed criminals. Forty of them were released before time. Those who show marked improvements are also rewarded, both materially and spiritually. Those who do not do their work, refuse to be reformed through labor, or try to commit sabotage or to escape are duly punished for their criminal acts. Tu Shih-chin, a secret agent of the KMT who led six criminals in their escape and was arrested along with them, was brought back to the farm and shot before a gathering of all inmates.

The article is an excellent example of Chinese journalism today. I have reproduced the article at such length, for between its lines appears the real news of resistance, forced labor and suicides. The newspapers no longer print news. They are expected to be a propaganda agency of the state.

I was, however, prepared to accept what the article claimed. But before doing so, I told my interpreter that I would like to see one of the "farms," and two other journalist colleagues in the Delegation joined in the request. It was met with silence. At a roadside railway station, while we were, I think, on our way to Canton from Shanghai, I saw a long line of prisoners, about two hundred in number, roped together in pairs, waiting to be transferred. Our train came to a stopping point a distance from the prisoners.

I was anxious to know who they were, so I rushed up to the official in charge and asked. He said he had seen nothing, though this was hardly possible. I described the prisoners but his only reply was "Maybe."

The danger of counterrevolution seems to be ever present; at least its threat is publicized with a view to the elimination of all opposition elements within the country. Since the Common Program is the fundamental law of the state, any opposition, nonacceptance or criticism is tantamount to treason. Terror is dictatorship's most effective weapon and Communist China utilizes its power to compel submission. Concentration camps, the disappearance of people in the middle of the night, suicides, public trials and public murders are a common feature of daily life.

While I was in Peking I heard of another trial involving three Italians, one German, one French, one Japanese and one Chinese. They were accused of conspiracy to blow up the Tien An Man on October 1, 1950, and with it all the leaders of the Republic. They were all supposed to have been spies and agents of a "Fascist Japanese, Chinese and United States government." One of them was a Catholic bishop and a delegate of the Papal Nuncio. The charge sheet against them sounds fantastic and all of them are, as usual, supposed to have confessed.

Like the Moscow Trials, these confessions are "the last refinement of terror with the victims forced to hymn paeans to their executioners." * The "conspirators" were arrested on September 26, 1950, and for eleven months the Security Police grilled them. Their case was then transferred to the Procurator's office and they were tried by a Military Court and sentenced on August 17, 1951. These

* Leslie Paul, *Age of Terror.*

dates have some relation to the Chinese entry in the Korean
War. It will be recalled that in September, 1950, China
decided to intervene. The armistice negotiations at Kaesong
were deadlocked and broke down on August 23, 1951. I
was given in Peking a copy of the indictment and the ver-
dict. It is difficult to judge the guilt of the accused from
these papers but the few documents which are published as
having been found with the accused do not convince me as
to their genuineness. I shall reproduce one letter which the
Chinese claimed established a link between the U.S. Military Attaché and the chief accused:

Peking
29 November 1949

Dear Tony,

Please you and Y come to my place on Hsi Pial Pei Hutung
on Friday 2 December at 12:45 for luncheon. Mr. Clubb has
accepted an invite to be there.

Ask Y please to excuse me if I save time and trouble by not
sending him a separate invite.

I am nervous about your sending classified material to me by
chit. Do you think this is O.K.? One letter taken from your
boy might make a world of trouble for us both.

The stuff is most valuable and I am so glad to have it.

Sincerely,
Dave.

I could not believe this letter to have been written by
anyone whose mother tongue was English. It sounds
Chinese. The trial and conviction have had a far-reaching
significance for they involved all the foreigners resident in
China and particularly the Roman Catholic clergy. Not
much is known about the tribulations of the missionaries.

THE GREAT PEACE

Many of the missions had enjoyed extraterritorial rights and a simple note from the mission had often helped the Chinese Christians to win a case in the court. The Roman Catholic clergy came in for much more attack than others. The visit of Cardinal Spellman to Yu Pin, the adviser to Chiang, and the consequent organization of the League of Mary, had been interpreted as counterrevolutionary activity. It is said that the Roman Catholics were advised that communism was a threat to religion and that as such they should resist it. The Catholic Church itself did not actively participate in the resistance, but its influence led it to be associated with the spearhead of the movement. It was an unfortunate mixup, for the Chinese Communists who had not interfered with religion up to then found in it justification for the persecution of the clergy.

I heard in Peking and Nanking the gruesome details of fantastic charges leveled against orphanages conducted by nuns. In one case the older inmates of an orphanage came to testify against the nuns but the younger children, who could not yet be taught, testified that the nuns had treated them with love and affection. There are many such stories all over China and they puzzled me, for they gave me a feeling of being in a country which was deliberately fanning the hatreds of war.

Today some seventy foreigners are rotting in Chinese prisons, not knowing what their crimes may be. There will be no fair trial nor opportunity for them to defend themselves. Article 7 of the Common Program has enjoined that all counterrevolutionaries who oppose the cause of People's Democracy—communism—must be suppressed. All accusations must be cross-checked and "loose ends will be tied up." I came across one such cross-checking in Shanghai. A

192

worker in one of the electrical works was accused of counterrevolution. His fellow workers, who had a grudge against him, were called upon to testify against him. The only evidence which "tied up" the charges was that he listened to the Voice of America broadcasts.

This is the fate of the people who are accused of being counterrevolutionaries and spies. But what of the common man? Does the rule of law prevail in his case? One of the fundamental principles of democracy is that the rights of the individual are protected by law. In China the individual has no rights except as a member of a group. His contractual rights are limited to his relations with the state. It is the state as organized under the Common Program which counts and not the individual. The Judiciary is therefore a handmaid of the Executive and not independent of it. Thus, the Chief Justice of the Supreme Court is a member of the government and is often employed to carry out political missions. The law is governed by politics and not by any considerations of justice.

Knowledge of law is not required of the judges in the courts, and the judges of the People's Courts which I attended in Peking, Nanking and Shanghai had little familiarity with the concept of law. They were only persons in whose political loyalty the state had confidence. These courts followed no formal procedure, and had no back cases for precedents. They are singularly bare of books. There are no lawyers to prosecute or to defend. The tribunals are made up of a presiding magistrate, a representative of the class organization to which the accused belonged and a recorder. All the old laws have been abrogated and today only the Marriage Law, the Trade Union Law and the Land Reform Law, together with the Common Program, form the basic laws of the state. The public present in the court is allowed to take part in the proceedings and come forward as witnesses or hurl accusations and call for severe punishments.

In Peking I attended a divorce case in the People's Court. A woman with three children had asked for a divorce on grounds of ill-treatment by her husband. The court appealed to the husband to think over the matter. "Think if you have any feudalistic ideas. You should help your wife to educate herself and improve her cultural level instead of ill-treating her. If you have any chauvinistic ideas get rid of them." The couple withdrew their case.

In Nanking it was a case of murder. It was alleged that the mother-in-law had driven the daughter-in-law to suicide. The father-in-law was accused of being a henpecked husband and not preventing the ill-treatment of the deceased daughter-in-law. One brother-in-law and two sisters-in-law of the deceased were also charged with ill-treating the deceased. The case had created considerable public interest, and a large crowd resident in the area where the accused lived had come to the court. The magistrate read out the charges and the evidence in the case. Then the members of the public came forward and accused the persons facing the trial. Their evidence was limited to some incidents of ill-treatment which they had heard of because of their proximity. They were not cross-examined by the accused, who were permitted only to deny the evidence produced. Ultimately, the father-in-law broke down and confessed that his wife had ill-treated the deceased. The representative of the Democratic Women's Organization then addressed the court on social reform, status of women and family life. After this, the magistrate sentenced all the accused persons. The old mother-in-law was sentenced to fifteen years of imprisonment, and the father-in-law to two years for being henpecked!

In Shanghai it was also a murder trial. The accused was known as a "tigress" and was charged with killing her maidservant. The crime had been committed in Kuomintang days and she had been acquitted by the police then. Now the whole story was raked up again and willing neighbors had come forward to testify against her. The charge sheet included such statements as that her son had been a Japanese informant and a Kuomintang spy. These statements had no relevance to the actual crime but perhaps were brought up because the woman was a possible counterrevolutionary. There was no cross-examination. The accused simply denied the evidence.

These trials convinced me that in China the roles of the prosecution and the judge are combined. For an individual accused of any crime the difficulties are multiplied many times because he is presumed to be guilty till he proves his innocence. Since there is no rule of law, the individual has no chance of justice based on evidence.

3

SAN FAN WU FAN

IT was at Canton on the very first day of my return to China that I came across a new tidal wave which had been sweeping down from the North over the whole country. Along the streets I noticed its powerful impact on the many shops closed with official seals that announced they had been "law-breaking" businesses. Across the canal which divides the old British Concession from the city, I saw a crowd of people shouting slogans in front of a small shop. I walked over to the scene from the Victory House, accompanied by my omnipresent interpreter, and waited on the edge of the crowd. Inside the shop, in the middle of the floor, the shopkeeper kneeled with his hands behind his back and eyes cast down in humble submission to his employees. "What is happening here?" I asked. "A meeting" was the cryptic reply. "What sort of a meeting?" I could learn nothing more.

I came across it again the same morning on the river-side road under the shade of a tree. A group of young boys and girls, with exercise books and pencils in their hands, were engaged in a serious discussion. I stood around and talked to them. They were students from a school on the other side of the town studying the Anti-Three and Anti-Five, the San Fan Wu Fan, I was told. They were discussing corruption, bureaucracy and waste. "Isn't it waste," I asked, "to leave your studies at the school and sit here to study waste?" "The school is closed; besides this is our patriotic duty," someone answered. My interpreter was put out by my questions and suggested we move on.

I saw it again and again in Canton that day. Processions of boys and girls, of workers in shops and factories, constantly marching with flags flying to the beat of the drum. Often it was the Yang-ko drum, the drum of the harvest dance, which has all the rhythm and passion of far-off Africa. Everywhere the march went on, and some few found suicide more bearable than the inexorable retribution which was overtaking them for their alleged crimes of bribery and corruption. It was, the Chinese said, the moral rearmament of the country and the Party against ancient traditions of the "squeeze." It had the fervor of a confessional which purifies and the politics of self-criticism which purges.

In early 1951 some activities of the Party members in the Ju Chwan country in the province of Kiangsi had been discovered to be undesirable. The head of the police and the member in charge of propaganda, together with a large number of Party members, were found corrupt and dissipated. They were therefore expelled from the Party. In April a small conspiracy among officials of the revenue department was unearthed. Some thirty-one minor officials or Kanpus had embezzled about seven billion yuans (one million yuans = sixteen pounds = forty-five dollars). These cases were followed by others. In the Ministry of

Communication seventeen Kanpus had embezzled eight billion yuans and in East China another group of officials had misappropriated twenty billion yuans. Thus evidence was growing that all was not well with the Party. The thousands of new members in the Party had watered down its ideological strength. Obviously the sudden conquest of power had bred complacency and weakness. The revolutionary zeal which thrives on struggle was ebbing and a yearning for the comforts of life reared up the ugly head of corruption which had afflicted Chinese society so long.

"The Communist Party," according to Liu Shao-chi, "represents the brightest and the most progressive side of contemporary society. Gathered together in the Communist Party are the world's most conscious progressive and sound persons with the highest sense of morality and righteousness." But the Party no longer appeared to be so pure and so moral. There were many whispers and much uneasiness in the country and something drastic had to be done. Liu points the way how to carry on: "In addition to waging struggles against all dark and backward influences and things in society, we must carry on an inner-Party struggle to oppose the wavering, unsteady elements who reflect in the Party all kinds of dark and backward things in society. . . . In the course of prolonged struggles, we seek to educate, criticize, steel and reform those comrades who possess erroneous ideologies but who are not incorrigible."

The need for a large-scale purge was pointed out by Kao Kang, the cold-blooded and incorruptible Party puritan, Vice-Chairman of the Central People's Government and the Chairman of the Northeast People's Government. Addressing the Party leaders of Manchuria in August, 1951, he said:

"Rightist views are to be seen in the misunderstanding as to economic trends in the villages after the land reform. Now that villages are improving under land reform, some comrades consider that because the peasants will inevitably grow stronger and a division into classes will inevitably arise, it is not necessary to organize the peasant production on the line of mutual aid and still less necessary to raise the agricultural mutual aid groups to higher planes of agricultural co-operatives. Some comrades think we cannot put a proper limit at the present time on the spontaneous growth of the peasant power. They fail to realize that the duty of the village Party members is to promote agricultural mutual aid and agricultural co-operatives and bring the peasants gradually step by step along the road to collectivization. On the contrary they imagine that after the villages begin to get better off, the duty of the village Party members is to hire laborers and to become rich peasants.

"This attitude," he continued, "denies the role of the peasants as the most reliable of the working class; it results in the working class abandoning its role of leadership of the peasantry; it denotes weakness and surrender to the increased capital element in the villages."

Mao Tse-tung followed Kao in his address to the third session of the People's Political Consultative Conference in October, 1951, by stressing the need for economy, increased production and ideological remolding, and he blamed the capitalists or the national bourgeoisie for infiltrating into the Party and corrupting it with their "sugar-coated shells of bribery." He said, "At the close of the second session of the National Committee, I suggested the use of criticism and self-criticism for self-education and remolding. Now this suggestion has been gradually put into practice. The remolding of ideology, primarily the ideological remolding of the various types of intellectuals, is an important condition for the thorough carrying out of democratic reforms in various fields and the gradual carrying out of industrialization in our country. Therefore let us hope there will be still greater success in the steady progress of this self-education movement."

So began the great struggle in the Party to purify the ideologically defective and to weed out corrupt members. The movement was called San Fan or Anti-Three and was initiated in the government. The process was inherent in Communist theory. All high officials were called upon to volunteer self-criticism and confessions, while accusations and explanations followed from other officials who were their subordinates and could offer evidence to support their charges. For four months the whole administration was at a standstill while the Kanpus were engaged in this heart-searching examination in protracted departmental meetings. The accused were denied even the right of silence and orgies of petty questionings and confessions followed. The Minister of Justice confessed she was fond of flowers and put some flowers in her office daily at the expense of the state. Even Mao and Chou appeared before their respective councils and criticized themselves for past mistakes. By January, 1952, it was found that 1,670 officials in 27 departments of the government were corrupt. They were called upon to confess all their sins and many who confessed were deemed "not incorrigible" and let off with fines and light punishments. Others who refused to confess, or against whom very serious charges were leveled, were sentenced to death, or fined so heavily that penury resulted. The staff of the Bank of China was found to be receiving about 10 million yuans from merchants for supplying economic intelligence. In Tientsin top-ranking Party members Lin Ching-sha and Chang Tze-shan were sentenced to death. As secretaries of the Tientsin office of the Party they had misappropriated about 153 billion yuans of public funds meant for refugee relief and for the construction of the port. A public trial was held in Peking on February 1st when seven leading officials and Party members were tried by the people. The accused included Sung Teh-kuai, the director of the administrative office of the Central Ministry of Public Security, Mau Yen, the departmental director of the Health Bureau of the Ministry of Railways, and Lu Ta, departmental director of Steel Industry. A private capitalist of Shanghai, director of the Cheng Tai rubber factory, was included among the accused for swindling the government by overcharging it to the extent of millions of yuans.

In Shanghai, I saw the film of this public trial. A special showing was arranged for the Indian Delegation who had asked to see it. It was a scene reminiscent of the days when the tumbrels rumbled over the cobbled streets of Paris and the people jeered at the victims of the guillotine. On the stage sat the Chief Justice of China, an elderly international jurist; Po Yi-po, the Minister of Finance; the Chairman of the Central Austerity Inspection Department; and the man who organized the first guerrilla resistance. In front were the seven victims, facing the crowd. They were brought in by armed men who stood behind them once they had taken their places. The victims stood with their eyes looking on the ground and their hands behind their backs. From their shoulders hung long streamers reaching to their feet describing them as criminals and traitors. The crowd of men and women sat quietly waiting for their cues to hurl abuse and insults at the victims.

Po Yi-po in his charge asserted that the loss to the state from the activities of the accused amounted to as much as 45 million dollars. "This could have bought 18 million catties of food grains and helped to feed 280,000 men for a whole year, or China could have purchased 66 fighter planes for the defense against American imperialism." Loud and prolonged shouts called for the blood of the traitors.

Po Yi-po continued: "If the corruption spread to the whole country on this scale, the people would be deprived of capital which would be enough to set up 10 modernized factories each employing 2,000 to 3,000 men and set back the industrial progress of the country." He then spoke of the evidence against each defendant and described their heinous crimes against the people. The speech was interrupted repeatedly by shouts for direct retribution from the audience. The shouting appeared to be prearranged and the cries were taken up by one corner, then another, till the crowd was whipped into a furious mob. Radio, telephones and cinemas were impressed into the service of this fury and people phoned from their homes to the court asking for the death penalty.

According to the Communist theory the law courts are instruments of mass condemnation. "The judgment must come as a climax to mass mobilization so that when the sentence is passed masses will rise in fury against the accused." The purpose of such public trials is to strike terror and let loose the forces of mob passion against the "enemy." After Po Yi-po sat down, the crowd shouted and screamed for the blood of the victims offered to them. They threw rotten eggs, tomatoes and stones at their prey, who could not lift their faces and look at the crowd or the judges. There was no examination of the accused and they were given no chance to reply to the charges. The Chief Justice got up and sentenced two of the accused to death, four to varying terms of imprisonment, and released one who immediately went and sat in the crowd and joined in the denunciation of those found guilty.

Thus began the Terror. Peng Chen, the Mayor of Peking, was put in charge of the whole campaign. The San Fan was directed against corruption, waste and bureaucracy, which includes not only red tape but also a "bourgeois pattern of conduct"—indifference to work, ostentatious living and a sense of separation from the masses. The method used was confession, criticism and self-criticism and finally a public trial and an accusation.

The Peking trial was followed by similar trials in Tientsin, Nanking, Wuhan, Shanghai and elsewhere. Fantastic charges were leveled and exemplary punishments were meted out. Seven Kanpus in Ching Hsi county of Kiangsi province were demoted for marrying daughters of "reactionary antirevolutionary landlords." An official was charged with wasteful expenditure on clothes to impress the foreign delegations visiting China during the October 1, 1951 celebrations. (As a member of the Indian Delegation then, I saw no ostentatious display of finery.) One official was denounced by his chauffeur for using the car to take his lady friend home from a dance. In Shanghai sixteen Party office-bearers were dismissed for Party lapses. The secretary of the Party was found guilty of living in a palatial mansion with a swimming pool. Another official was charged with "dissipation such as building a private garden, going to private dancing halls and lewdly playing with females." Another was accused of putting up a notice on the office bulletin about the loss of his fountain pen and receiving five Parker 51's from brokers who did business with the office.

For four months the infant administration of China was shaken to its roots. No work was done while the Kanpus were engaged in this bout of self-purification. The effects of this moral rearmament were visible when I returned to China. No official was willing to make a decision. Everything was referred to the higher-ups and there was more centralization of authority and a marked deterioration in efficiency. All manner of delays took place. The arrangements for the Indian Cultural Delegation were confused and slack. No replies were given to its requests until the Peking Foreign Office was consulted. The difference between my two visits was so great that it could not go unnoticed.

But the San Fan had wider implications than mere correction of the Party and the administration. The existence of external influences on the Kanpus was continuously being brought to the fore. The inclusion in the February 1st trial of a private capitalist was also a pointer and a warning to those influences. Communist theory has repeatedly stressed that the inner Party struggle is only a reflection of the outer class struggle.

Liu Shao-chi, the lean and wan-looking Party intellectual and theoretician, whose main task was to co-ordinate Maoism with Stalinism and show that there were no differences between the two, had foreseen the danger as far back as 1941. He then wrote, "Right from the day of its birth, our Party had never for a single moment lived in any environment but that of serious struggle. The Party and the proletariat have constantly lived inside the encirclement of various nonproletariat classes such as the big bourgeoisie, the petty bourgeoisie, the peasantry and even the remnants of the feudal forces. All these classes, when they are struggling against the proletariat or when they are co-operating with it, utilize the unstable elements within the Party and the proletariat to penetrate into the heart of the Party and the proletariat, and constantly influence the Party and the proletariat in ideology, in living habits, in theory and in action." He therefore concluded that the inner Party struggle is a reflection of the class struggle outside.

In July, 1949, addressing the Communist Party, Mao said, "Who are the people? At the present stage in China they are the working class, the peasantry, the petty bourgeoisie and the national bourgeoisie." The unity of these classes was essential to build the democratic dictatorship for if "the things were not done like this the revolution would fall, the people would suffer and the state would perish." This unity of classes was the People's Front which the European world knows well. Now that the revolution had succeeded, the unity was impeding the Communists and they needed the wealth of the bourgeoisie to remedy their economic difficulties. Politically they wanted a proletarian revolution to establish their dictatorship and break down all the social defenses of Chinese society which had for centuries believed in Taoist individualism.

Between the revolution and the building up of a stable state came the temporary state of artificial unity achieved by a desperate people to end the Kuomintang rule. The San Fan Wu Fan movements mark the end of the democratic revolution of 1949 and the establishment of a Communist state. A parallel lies in the ousting of the Mensheviks by the Bolsheviks.

Into this struggle were poured all the resources of the state. Newspapers, radio, films, mass trials, processions, meetings and slogans were impressed into service, and shop workers, factory hands, housewives, sons and daughters, domestic servants and students were called upon to testify against employers, parents, husbands and professors.

The February 1st trial was a grave warning to the national bourgeoisie. The first reaction to the threat was the idea of a league for attack and defense, but the merchants of Shanghai and Tientsin well knew what would follow any such resistance. Instead, in a mood of fear they started on their own initiative the Wu Fan (Anti-Five) in order to remove some untrustworthy elements from among them. What followed was anything but a mere weeding out of corrupt elements.

The Wu Fan was a war against five sins. These were: (1) bribery, (2) the stealing of government property, (3) cheating the government, (4) obtaining and using economic information for private speculation, and (5) tax evasion. Every shop, business house and factory had to go through a routine of confession, criticism and self-criticism. Committees were formed by different professions to examine their colleagues. Shops and business houses were divided into areas or districts and put under Austerity Inspection Committees. Confessions were sent to these committees and then the employees of the shop or business house concerned were asked to examine these confessions in the light of their own knowledge of their employers. Inquisitions of the employers were then held and sons, wives and servants came forward to testify and hurl real and imaginary charges at the bowed head of the victim.

In Tientsin, I came across a case of an old curio merchant. His shop was well known and before the revolution it had branches in major cities of the world. All these branches had gone their independent ways in time and the owner had little control over their affairs. This old man of more than seventy years was asked to submit the accounts of all the branches and pay the tax which he was accused of evading. He pleaded a valid inability to comply, but was thrown into prison and, one day, marched through the town with a rope round his neck and his hands tied behind his back. He was forced to carry a placard declaring he was a criminal. Soon thereafter, he was released on parole for one month, during which time he was again instructed to produce the accounts of his foreign branches or be prepared for a sentence of death. Helpless, he lay on his deathbed waiting to be carried away when the parole time was over.

In Shanghai a small shopkeeper who had purchased some $85 worth of stocks in a joint stock company was suffering for the folly of owning these shares. It was alleged that the managing director of the stock company had overcharged the state to the tune of several millions. The company was fined heavily and the stockholders were held liable on the ground that they had derived the benefit of the profits. This particular shopkeeper alone was called upon to pay $2,800 toward the liability of the company. He had no means of paying such a debt and was ultimately compelled to sell whatever he had, as quickly as possible, for every day's delay meant increase in the liability.

Outside the People's Bank in Shanghai I saw a mile-long

queue eager to sell their few gold possessions so that the heavy fines imposed on them could be paid. The queue was restive, for they had been waiting for days for their turn. Ultimately the government offered to receive their gold as a deposit against their indebtedness and then calculate its value when each case came up, with the payment considered made from the day of the deposit. In this manner all the savings of the bourgeoisie were expropriated and many of them were left in poverty, unable to continue their business.

In Tientsin, Shanghai and Canton, I heard that many businessmen, unable to bear the persecution or meet the fantastic demands made on their limited resources, had committed suicide. People jumped from their windows or drowned themselves in the river. It was not uncommon to hear the siren of the ambulance at any time of the day as it rushed to pick up the remains and hush all talk. In Shanghai the estimates of suicides varied from two hundred to two thousand, for no one could tell what happened in other parts of the city. In Canton I heard that at least five or six people were committing suicide daily.

Every firm which went through the Wu Fan was classified in one of five categories and accordingly certified. They were (1) law abiding, (2) fundamentally law abiding, (3) semi-law abiding, (4) law breaking and (5) completely law breaking. The firms of the second category were allowed to retain their undue gains if such gains did not exceed more than 2 million yuans ($90). Group three had to restore all such gains to the state. In category four all illegal gains had to be paid to the state and a fine was also demanded. Imprisonment and even sentence of death were included in the punishment of firms of the fifth category. A decree was issued on April 21, 1952, which laid down the punishments, ranging from one year to life imprisonment according to the amount involved. The seriousness of the crime was mitigated by (1) voluntary confession, (2) complete confession after initial discovery, (3) denouncing others and (4) youth.

The punishment in the San Fan aspect of the campaign was much more serious. It involved imprisonment, death and confiscation of property if the money embezzled amounted to more than 10 million yuans ($450).

I have a report of the investigations carried out in 4,000 firms by Municipal Austerity Investigations Committee of the Second Ward in Tientsin. It has been taken from the Chinese-English Intelligence of April 23, 1952, published in Tientsin. It reads in part:

In the course of the classified disposals of the industrial and commercial firms as made by the Committee, there were more than 4,000 firms that already completed the formalities in connection with the conclusive reports. According to what was revealed by the statistics available, there were 460 law-abiding firms, 2,672 fundamentally law-abiding firms, 84 semi-law-abiding law-breaking firms; in all there were 3,216 firms. Careful and minute calculations and computations are being made in connection with the remaining firms. Up to now the disposal of the three classes as mentioned above was fundamentally completed. There remained several tens of firms that had not yet been passed. Should they still be unwilling to make frank and honest confessions, they would have to receive the punishment which would be their due.

What I have seen is, I am sure, only a fringe of a vast upsurge which has overtaken the business and commercial classes of China who had largely contributed to the overthrow of Chiang and who had in a measure made the revolution possible. The people were mobilized and what has been called "democracy in action" let loose because in essence the Wu Fan movement is a class struggle waged by the party in power against its own people in an attempt to neutralize an entire class of people. The masses were roused in order to make them feel it was their decision which was being carried out. They themselves understood little of what was happening. But when passions are fanned, the mob feels the exhilaration of action and participation in vital changes affecting the country.

The immediate result of such a procedure, or self-criticism, individuals have stated, is something akin to renovation of one's outlook and beliefs. A dentist in Peking told me that when he confessed before his colleagues in the profession his misdeeds both as a professional and as a man, he felt himself light and happy. All the burdens of the past had been removed. A world-renowned Chinese professor of philosophy confessed that all his knowledge in the past had been wrong and his theory was harmful and false. Such catharsis understandably gives temporary relief from guilt, but it cannot achieve any permanent results except on the basis of terror which is instilled by the public confession. The place of God or conscience is taken by the "interests of the masses" and compels rigid discipline in all human contacts. Five embezzlers in the Ministry of Railways were revealed, in February, by the denunciations of their families. Human dignity has ceased to exist.

The movement which began with the need for a Party purge and the uncovering of corruption in the government grew into a mass struggle against the national bourgeoisie, and the virtual elimination of the latter. What effect this will have on the Chinese economy is still to be seen. The leaders realized that the movements had gone beyond what was originally intended to be only a purification of both the Party and society. Attempts were therefore made in April to conclude them. The May Day celebrations and the presence of many visitors provided an excuse to withdraw the campaign quickly.

There may have been other reasons for the unleashing of this "unmerciful struggle" at the present stage of the Chinese revolution. It is said that the Communists are convinced of an all-out war in the near future. China therefore feels the need for complete national unity and a purge of all potentially disloyal elements. Mao had called the national bourgeoisie "weak in character, lacking foresight and courage."

The San Fan Wu Fan campaigns have been given international significance by Chou En-lai and others in China. It is not quite clear what importance can be attached to this but it may be noted that the present campaigns were launched on February 1, 1952. On February 22 China followed them up by the charges of bacteriological warfare against the United States. Though apparently there is no connection between the two campaigns, they represent a double-pronged drive to unify the country internally and win as many supporters and fifth columns outside as possible, in case the world is plunged into a war.

4

GERM WARFARE

TOWARD the end of my second visit to Peking, I saw that the Indian Delegation was scheduled to visit the "war exhibition." I gave no thought to it, little realizing that the exhibition was concerned with the charges of "germ warfare" which have been so loudly proclaimed. It was therefore a welcome surprise to arrive there, because for the first time I was coming face to face with a question which the government had sought to make a world issue. The accusations of germ warfare were news and the exhibition was an attempt to convince the visitor that they were a fact.

The exhibition was in three parts. In the first section, an attempt was made to prove that the United States was actively engaged in the research of germ warfare. American military journals, scientific books and news magazines were shown discussing the problem and its possibilities. The news of the employment in Korea of Shiro Ishie and Jiro Wakanatsu, Japanese generals actively connected with the Japanese Research Department 731 at Harbin in 1935–36, was prominently displayed as a proof that General

Ridgeway was trying out methods of dropping diseased and infected insects.

The second section displayed the compartment bomb, parachuted cardboard containers, broken fragments of a porcelain bomb and shells alleged to have been dropped over North Korea and Manchuria containing infected flies, mosquitoes and other insects. There were photographs along the walls of the places where such bombs had been dropped. Some of the photographs also showed an investigating commission in white overalls, rubber boots and masks making "on-the-spot" investigations. These photographs were interesting because they gave the date on which the bombs had been dropped and the date when the investigation was carried out. One particular photograph drew my attention. It showed the Fushun Race Course where, it was stated, a bomb had been dropped in February, 1952, and which the investigating party had reached for an "on-the-spot" investigation with all the paraphernalia of masks and overalls on March 24.

In the corner of the room a wire recorder with a loud-speaker was playing the confessions of two American air-force men. They had been prisoners of war since January, 1952, when their plane had been shot down in Korea. In these recorded statements, Kenneth Enoch and John Quin declared that they had made repeated sorties over North Korea from January 4 to January 13, dropping a number of "duds" which they claimed were germ bombs. The statements gave details of training and lectures they had received on germ warfare previous to these dates and declared, "We don't think the American people would agree to the use of bacteriological warfare, but they don't know the facts." In a glass case nearby were the written statements by both of them allegedly in their own handwriting. The Chinese claimed that the statements conclusively proved their charges against the United States Army in Korea.

The third section displayed a series of microscopes with various bacteria cultures alleged to have been made from germs which included "beetles, bugs, flies, fleas, spiders, crickets, mosquitoes and other insects many of which were hitherto unknown in Korea." On the walls were displayed pictures and actual specimens of these germs. Included also were the photographs of three victims of plague, who were, it was stated, infected by flies dropped by the U.S. planes. This was followed by propaganda posters of the manner in which germ warfare was being countered.

Finally a large poster announced that between January 28 and March 31, 1952, 804 germ air raids over 70 cities and counties of Korea and North China had taken place. Every photograph or poster in the exhibition bore captions in three languages, Chinese, Russian and English. The Indian Delegation was conducted through every detail of the exhibition and guides read out each caption. It took more than three hours to go round and Mme. Pandit had to listen to each and every explanation patiently. The Chinese were obviously anxious that she should miss no detail. At the end of the visit, the Delegation was conducted to an adjoining room where, as was the Chinese custom, tea, fruits and cakes were served. At the table Mme. Li Teh-chuan, the Minister of Health who had personally conducted Mme. Pandit through the exhibition, welcomed the impressions of the Delegation. It was a delicate task and every interpreter who accompanied the members had been asked to listen for any comments made by the members.

Mme. Pandit, however, rose to the occasion and thanked the Health Minister for "showing the exhibition" to the Delegation.

That afternoon the foreign correspondents' liaison office rang me up and insisted that I should visit the germ warfare exhibition that same evening before its formal opening to the public. I pointed out that I had already seen it in the morning for almost four hours, but the liaison office would not take no for an answer. I was told that I must come and that there would be a press conference, where I could, if I so wished, ask questions. I knew the Chinese were anxious to know the reactions of the Delegation. They thought that through me they would be able to learn something about them and hence they insisted. I had no alternative but to go.

And what a press conference it was! I am certain that it was hastily called for my benefit so that I might reveal the reactions of the Indian Delegation. The whole Commission which had made the "on-the-spot" investigations was present. The Commission included many pathologists, entomologists and physicians and was presided over by Chou Shu-tung, Vice-Chairman of the China Peace Committee. There were representatives present of the Tass, Pravda, and Vietminh news agencies and a dozen or more Chinese reporters, besides Mme. Kung Peng, the head of the Department of Information and Research of the Ministry of Foreign Affairs.

Immediately on arrival the press representatives were asked to view the exhibition. I hesitated to go through it again but the liaison officer came up to me specially and asked me to come into the exhibition halls. Inside there were batteries of ciné cameras and arc lights to take moving pictures of the foreign newsmen going round. I was asked if I minded being filmed along with other correspondents. It was difficult to decline the request. How could I object to any publicity of the fact that I had seen the exhibition? But I told the liason officer that though I had no objections to any photographs being taken, I had no intention of going round again as I had already been through the exhibits.

The Chinese gave up the idea of filming me with the others as they viewed the displays, so I wandered around picking out some special exhibits in order to refresh my memory. I knew this was a most significant collection which could affect the relations between the West and the East for generations to come. Hiroshima had left bitter memories in the minds of many Asians, and another similar attempt on any Asian country, whatever its justification, would confirm the suspicions of many people that to the West the life of an Asian was of no value, nor worthy of any consideration. My morning visit had convinced me that the exhibition proved nothing. The various bacteriological specimens could have been produced in a laboratory. The investigations were superficial and carried out by a prejudiced party. It is true that the statements of Enoch and Quin, giving minute details of air sorties, previous preparations, and instructions and training given to the American air force, raised some doubts. But I was also convinced that General Ridgeway and the United States knew well the folly of any such attempt, quite apart from its human considerations.

In the midst of my wandering, Mme. Kung Peng came up to me. She was one of those intense women one so often comes across in the Communist hierarchy. As the head of the Information Department of the Foreign Ministry she had acquired a reputation for taciturnity. She was unusually tall for a Chinese and the pallor of her face framed by neatly brushed black hair added sternness to her personality. I believe she had been to India during the war and was familiar with many other countries. She spoke English fluently but only when it served her purpose. Otherwise the usual interpreter was always present. I was a little surprised that instead of my seeking after her she had sought me out. I knew then that I was to go through an examination. This could only be done in English and she decided to use it. "I have been very busy though I wanted to see you very much," she said. "What do you think of the exhibition?" I was not ready for so direct a question, so I talked about the necessity of convincing the neutral countries of Asia and gaining their sympathies for China. This, I told her, could only be done in two ways. Either China must place before the Asian countries the facts of the sufferings of the North Koreans and the Chinese by disease and epidemics brought about by germ warfare, or a report by an independent and impartial commission must be presented to them for their information. There was no third way.

But Mme. Kung was ready with her questions. She said, "Is not the evidence of Enoch and Quin sufficient to convince any genuine inquirer?"

I flung caution to the wind and answered, "No, a prisoner of war is under duress and any statement made by him cannot be accepted as made of free will."

"But we treat our prisoners of war well," she replied. "Enoch and Quin made their statements entirely of their own will. They did so because they realized they were fighting an unjust war."

"It may be so, Mme. Kung," I said. "But I too was once a political prisoner in the days of our struggle for India's freedom. I know what prison means, however good the treatment may be."

Mme. Kung suddenly became stiff and official. She asked me whether I intended to ask any questions when the press conference began later that evening, and to let her know in advance what those questions were. I had not thought of my questions at all. This was the first press conference I was attending in China and I did not know the procedure. I was hoping some statement would be made during the conference which would give me an opportunity to ask for further information. But Mme. Kung's request made it clear that I had to tell her beforehand what I wanted to know. Otherwise I might as well not have come. I told her that I was only a newsman and my questions have nothing to do with what I believe or do not believe. It was my job to find out what the readers in my country would be interested in knowing. Therefore, I said, would the Commission tell me what was implied when it said it had carried out "on-the-spot" investigation; what were the effects *in* China of the alleged germ warfare; and whether China was prepared to accept investigation of the "evidence" by an independent authority. I also told her that I would understand if my second query was not answered, if it were regarded as seeking information on what was a military secret.

Mme. Kung bowed sternly and left me to wander around. She went to the room where the members of the Commission were waiting for the press to finish its survey of the exhibition. The press came in after almost two hours and then the business of the evening commenced. I was hungry, for I had had no dinner, but there was no way to escape from the coming storm. I nibbled at a piece of cake, sipped tea and waited in a corner with my interpreter from the Liaison Office. The battery of ciné cameras and arc lights followed the press into the conference room and arrangements were made to take films of the proceedings. I was asked to sit next to the President, Chou Shu-tung, while the others sat where they liked.

Chou made a short speech saying that, though the United States had tried to deny the charges, the evidence which was placed before us should convince any observer that the charges were well founded in facts. He then called upon me to seek any information I wanted from the Commission. I was conscious that merely to put my questions bluntly would be misunderstood and involve me in many difficulties. So I explained why I was asking these questions: I said I wanted to carry out my job as efficiently as I could and hence my questions need not necessarily represent my views. I then stated the three questions which I had already put to Mme. Kung and stressed that they need not reply to the second question.

After my questions, the Tass agency man got up and asked, "If the insects found were of a type which is not found in China, where did they come from?" The Viet-minh representative merely expressed his solidarity with the Chinese people in their struggle against American "imperialism." The rest of the Chinese reporters asked whether the insects found had affected the crops, animals and vegetation. All the questions were noted down and the conference again adjourned.

After half an hour the Commission returned. Then followed a torrent of speeches by every member of the Commission, full of violence and anger against me for daring to question what "on-the-spot investigation" meant. It seemed to them that I was questioning their bonafides, their facts as presented in the exhibition and the insufficiency of proof. Perhaps nothing like this had ever happened in Communist China where the monotonous cry of "I believe" is all that is expected. In the heat of the moment no one bothered to translate the speeches into Russian. I was the object and all speeches were translated into English.

Mr. Liu Shao-chi, the Vice-Chairman of the Commission, Mme. Li, the Minister of Health and the Chairman of the Red Cross, Dr. Liu, the entomologist, Dr. Jung, a doctor of tropical medicine, Dr. Pen Chi-yu, professor of pathology, and many others spoke to me. They angrily reiterated that their investigation had been carried out by the Commission visiting the bombed spots in person, meeting people in the area and collecting material evidence.

"If you want proof that germs were dropped on the Commission investigating, then we have an actual incident when on April 2, Professor Wei Shi and a British correspondent of the *Daily Worker* had germs dropped on them while they were going round the field." The name of the *Daily Worker* correspondent brought a smile to my face. My question had had nothing to do with how the investigations were carried out, but with a photograph which showed me men in white overalls and rubber boots one month after the bombing incident investigating the area as if they were looking for germs.

The members of the Commission said angrily they would never tell what effect the germ warfare had had on

North Korea or on Northeast China, for "that is exactly what the Americans would like to know." The Americans, they insisted, continued the germ warfare right through the months of January to June. I am convinced that even if the United States Army had carried through a "tryout" from misunderstood orders, they would not have continued it as was stated by the Chinese. Public opinion in the United States and in Asia would have been alienated. Democracy cannot face such a prospect. There would have been a far greater possibility of convincing the people of Asia if the Chinese charges were not so wild and inflated. The very exaggeration had laid the Chinese case bare as propaganda and nothing else.

My main question, however, was whether the Chinese would accept an independent investigation. The Investigating Commission claimed that the Chinese Peace Committee had already suggested the need for an independent commission. Such a commission had been appointed by the International Democratic Lawyers and it was expected that the Peace Committee would be sending another commission composed of international scientists. The Vice-Chairman asserted that the Chinese people would welcome such an investigation if they had confidence in their impartiality. "Whatever this commission may be, it must be fair, just and unbiased. It must consider all facts." Although my question had particularly referred to the Chinese misgivings about the impartiality of the International Red Cross, I had also stated that investigations by the Peace Council or similar organizations were equally open to lack of confidence by the neutral peoples of the world.

The Press Conference lasted till midnight and I was hungry and tired. It had been to no purpose except perhaps to provide an opportunity for the members of the Commission to demonstrate their complete loyalty before the assembled journalists. I was thankful that the liaison officer was kind enough to send me back home in a car.

A few days after this I was informed that Mr. Kuo Mo-jo, the Chairman of the Peace Council and the Vice-Premier of China, would receive me. I had sent in my questions more than two weeks before the scheduled interview. I have a suspicion that the interview was granted because of my questions at the Press Conference.

I had asked whether the Chinese Peace Council would agree to an independent commission to inquire into the charges of germ warfare. I had further suggested that an independent commission would have to be an impartial commission and since it was difficult to determine the impartiality of persons, the only method possible was to appoint persons acceptable to both sides.

Kuo Mo-jo received me in his private home. In the sitting room there was a large panel of a painting of red dahlias by Chi Pei-she. It revealed Kuo Mo-jo's love of art and culture. He was not only a poet but one of the leading archeologists of China. He is famed for his polished speech and oratory. I heard him speak at the inauguration of the India-China Friendship Association and though I could understand nothing, his beautiful intonation, soft voice and gentle manners captivated me.

He spoke of the impartial commission I had asked about. "If an individual or a scientist or a lawyer sees, for example, a piece of cake and is prepared to state what he saw, he is in our opinion an impartial individual. Scientists who know black is black and who have no prejudices that prevent them from saying so are welcome to investigate the charges. Today too many people see black and call it gray. We believe, however, that there are many scientists, lawyers and tourists whose minds are like a mirror ready to reflect the reality. We think such people should organize the commission, but such people are not neutral, they are on the side of righteousness. A person is not impartial because a small group of people call him such. He must be so judged by the world opinion and the world opinion is determined by the majority of the people of the world."

I interrupted to remind him that there was no way of knowing world opinion. The only way of forming an impartial commission was to name members acceptable to both sides.

Kuo Mo-jo brushed my interruption aside. "It is impossible to find a group of people who could be acceptable to both the countries. The Americans will never agree on a group of scientists which is acceptable to us. If the group speaks impartially and honestly, the President will never accept the report."

I again interrupted, "Would China accept a commission nominated by the Asian countries and composed of Asian nationals?"

"A commission of scientists is being appointed by the World Peace Council," said Kuo Mo-jo. "We shall welcome India's participation in its work."

And so what is called "black" must remain or be found black. The China which once saw many shades of black and white had definitely shut her eyes and was intent upon preaching the gospel of hate. I did not then realize that I would run into the germ warfare site during our visit to Mukden. On our way to Fushun to see the coal mines, a glimpse of the race course which had brought all the indignation of the Investigating Commission down on my head flashed by. I at once recognized it. The race course was lying unused and overgrown with weeds. A few cattle nosed around in the dirt heaps. There was no sign of the germ bomb which had invited "on-the-spot" investigation. I drew the attention of the interpreter to the concrete stands. My recognition of the spot led me into difficulties, for late that evening, on our way to Tientsin from Mukden, the authorities suddenly thought of our health certificates. We had to open our luggage on the train and hand them over. At midnight I was awakened and informed that I had no plague inoculation certificate and as such the authorities at Shanghai Kwan on the Great Wall would have to detain me. I could not enter China from Manchuria without such a certificate.

I lay awake the whole night thinking I had gone and put my foot into trouble. Despite the surveillance of the formidable interpreter allotted to me, I had crossed the bounds and now had to wait in a "quarantine." At three in the morning I was told that perhaps at the station I might be given an injection of plague vaccine and allowed to travel. After another two hours of sleeplessness, at Shanhaikwan, two doctors in white overalls waited for me with a syringe. They were fully dressed complete to masks on their mouths, but one of them fiddled with the needle with his bare hands. It took him some time to adjust the syringe and then with little ceremony he pushed it into my arm. He shoved at the pump and I know not a drop of the vaccine went into my system. Operation "Germ Warfare" was over and I went to sleep at last.

Some days later, on the eve of our departure from China, someone wondered during a conversation with the Chinese why the farce of inoculation had been carried out with glucose in a syringe which did not work. The Chinese replied, "We know the immunity given by the vaccine could begin only after ten days but we thought we would be able to watch the signs of any disease better if Hutheesing was with us than at Shanhaikwan. Besides, it was not glucose."

5

DICTATORSHIP

I LEFT Peking with much regret. The peonies were in
bloom and their fragrance filled the central park. But there
was nothing more to do. The face of Peking was inscrutable, and the men at the helm of affairs had repeatedly
asserted the glory that is "liberated" Cathay. They had
asked us to see for ourselves in the rest of the country the
truth of what they had said. So we left Peking in three
wagons-lits with a restaurant car all to ourselves.

The journey to six big towns of seaboard China could
tell us little more than we already knew. We could not
meet the people and talk to them. We were in a sealed
train, leading our own life and drinking interminable
glasses of beer to forget the monotony of repetition.
Through the windows of the small compartment we could
see the tireless peasant hard at work on the small bit of
land with his little son, or a woman carrying a heavy burden on a bamboo pole slung across her shoulders, and the
constant blue of their simple clothing. The wrinkled face
of this earth, which had nourished millions of men and,

226

often, swept them to destruction in a moment of fitful frenzy, lay before our eyes.

Once late in the evening the train stopped at a wayside crossing. The day was fast drawing to a close and across the horizon a thin line of men was silhouetted. Suddenly the day sprang to life again in the glow of a beautiful twilight, casting its radiance on a peasant family standing nearby. The good earth was cut with heavy ruts of the many cartloads that had trundled over it. The peasant family was resting on the roadside. Their blue garments contrasted with the golden sky and the deep brown of the earth. A donkey stood by harnessed to the plough. I knew then how man could have loved this earth and clung to it through all his trials.

From Peking we went to Tatung. It was a visit to the ancient cultural links between India and China. Here in the fifth century an Indian monk named Kekeya came to the court of Bei Wei, the Mongol chief who had established his dynasty here. Tatung remained a city of culture and political power for almost a thousand years and vied with Peking. Here, a few miles outside the town, Kekeya and his disciples began the excavation of the famous caves of Yungkang. The caves took almost fifty years and he carved out giant monoliths of Buddha in the traditional Gupta style of his mother country.

The Indians had traveled through Afghanistan and Central Asia bringing with them the influences of Persian and Greek art. Today we find the long chain of Buddhist caves from Ajanta in Central India to Bamian (Afghanistan), Sinkiang, Tun-huang and Yungkang, all indicating the route by which Buddhism traveled to China.

The caves are situated about ten miles from the town in

the midst of the low-lying hills of Shansi on the banks of a
gently flowing river. Fifty-feet-high Buddhas looked across
the valley with peaceful, calm eyes as I went past. Each of
them radiated serene knowledge on this beautiful day in the
white lilac-scented air. Here, too, was the Maitreya Buddha, the future Messiah on a lion throne. But the future he
had conceived had come to fruition in hatred, fear, arrogance and mad intolerance. For two thousand years India
and China had lived in peace and friendship, cultivating the
art of life. Now must this all be brushed aside in the name
of the common man, so that life may become a prison?
Millions have been sacrificed so that the few in their self-
seeking greed might arrogate to themselves all the power.
It is the tragedy of our times that China, a country so im-
bued with the spirit of tolerance and understanding, should
have herself become a victim of ruthless intolerance. But I
was dreaming of the China that had taught us so many
things. Now it was all different.

The old idols were cast away and many had been carried
off by the Japanese Occupation Army. Their place had
been taken by the new "Saving Star" of China. Tatung
was a coal town where the famous coal mines had once
produced thousands of tons of coal. Today along the road
a straggling train of mules carrying a few chunks of coal
was wending its way from the mines. That evening at the
Municipal Banquet, I heard again the raucous strident voice
of New China. From "nirvana" to anti-Americanism was a
far cry. I cannot believe that the common man in China
has accepted this new gospel.

The journey from Tatung to the Great Wall was a
journey backward in human history. Thousands of men
had paid with their lives to build this wonder of the world

as a defense against aggression. But the Wall had proved of little use. Many invaders had come and established their rule. Today, the invader was inside the wall and men's freedom was at ransom. A lonely sentinel of the Liberation Army stood on guard facing the vast expanse of Manchuria. He seemed the symbol of New China which no longer hid behind the Wall but was marching out to unite Asia and the world. It was aggressive China which had after years of imperialist enslavement shaken off its shackles only to seek to fasten them upon others.

Sitting on the Wall among a group of visitors from other lands, we talked of the wasted human endeavor which had gone into the building of the Wall. We sang songs of our individual countries—songs of freedom and peace and liberation. Here was a monument to the fact that men do not live in freedom unless freedom is so enshrined in their hearts that they will willingly give up all to guard it. Big armies cannot defend it; they only wreck it. And in these ruins before us, it lay crushed under the weight of centuries.

The journey to Mukden followed the blockhouses which were constant reminder of the wars in this disputed territory. The Japanese, the Russians, the Kuomintang all had sought to exploit this rich country which is so essential to the economic life of China. The Manchus had once gone south to rule over Peking for centuries. Now the Southerners had come here to Mukden to add to the wealth of China. But all over Manchuria there was ample evidence of Russia. The hotel, the streets and many shops displayed their names in Russian. Pictures of Stalin and Mao hung together everywhere to remind viewers that without the help of the Russians, China could not go on.

THE GREAT PEACE

Mukden is a Japanese city with tall buildings and wide streets. On its cobbled road there was the constant rumble of mule carts bringing essential supplies. Occasionally a truck would tear down the street loaded with workers going to the factory. For the guests there were the latest models of American cars smuggled from across the sea.

And so to Tientsin, a Western city cut away from the rest of the country by the British, the French and many others. Today, it wears a Chinese look among a population which is sullenly silent. Its beautiful shops have no buyers and the few foreigners who remain cluster in the municipal café to drink tea and eat French pastry, waiting for the day when their exit permits grant them the liberty to go.

Nanking was a city of the past in spite of its modern avenues and palaces. Chiang had lived here for a long time but had refused to see the signs of his defeat in a society which was collapsing out of greed, inefficiency and the inability to exercise its power for the benefit of the people. The palace of Chiang at Nanking, with its many courtyards and tea gardens and red-latticed corridors, was lying bare and empty as a reminder that it would never again be occupied. Sun Yat-sen's 1911 revolution sought to free China from feudalism and Western imperialism. But the Kuomintang Nationalists were never able to achieve it "because they never completely smashed the rural authorities but compromised with them, never broke completely with Western imperialism, but depended on it." So Chiang was driven out. He will never return to China. On the domed walls of the Sun Yat-sen memorial the flag of his party no longer flies. It is replaced by the Red flag and a new dynasty has arisen which has sought its communion in the bloodstained stones of the Martyr's Hill. Nanking's beautiful parks are empty and the streets wear a woebegone face. Nanking is dead.

The memorial is beautiful. It commands a magnificent panoramic view of the valley around. Its simple architecture and the broad steps that lead up to it from the foot of the hill, the blue-tiled roofs of its gates and the evergreen avenues of the park around, suggest a nation's homage to the Three Principles which died with their founder only to provide a legend for the succeeding dictatorship. One Indian visitor exhibited deep emotion when we visited the tomb in October, 1951, in the mistaken idea that the People's Democracy believed in Dr. Sun Yat-sen. He spoke repeatedly of the greatness of Sun Yat-sen at various receptions in Nanking. Such tributes were too much for the Communists. The visitor was requested not to refer to him again. "We hold Dr. Sun Yat-sen in esteem," they told him, "but we do not like his name to be made much of in public."

Shanghai was undergoing the slow torture of a painful death when we came there. It was once an empire, separate from the rest of the country, where foreign millionaires and runaway gangsters jostled with each other in domineering splendor. Along its bund, the huge piles of imperialistic greed stand, now mausoleums of past exploitation of the "coolie." In the French concession and along the Nanking road the fashionable shops still display their faded finery for the few foreigners. There is no trade and its once crowded wharves and banking houses shelter only the men who could not be discharged. Its unmanageable traffic is slowed down by hundreds of pedicabs.

Shanghai is a city with no future. Many of its industries, it is said, have been transferred to the hinterland, leaving the millions of inhabitants bereft of any trade. Thousands of men and women, clad in foreign clothes instead of blue cotton uniforms, are waiting for the Tuesday morning when the newspaper may perhaps bring them the happy news of an exit permit. After the drabness of Peking it was good to see Chinese women in beautiful brocades, with smart coiffures and painted lips which brightened their ivory pallor. But fear lurked in their eyes, yearning for the right to live. I have never seen so many haunted faces.

Shanghai was a big prison house. I could not bear to remain here. The Communists were peasants and in their anxiety to avoid failure in the big cities, they had gone to the other extreme. They feared that these cities would harbor counterrevolutionaries who would by their long experience and authority dominate the peasant cadres and corrupt them. The San Fan showed that corruption could not be eradicated from a bureaucracy and overcentralized administration, so they have set themselves to destroy these cities. The proclaimed faith in new democracy had to be put aside by the very logic of communism. They have had to rely increasingly on the indoctrination of the young, brainwashing of the old, spying, confessions, self-criticism and liquidation.

This journey through China's big cities was a journey through brick-walled, impassive streets. We saw human faces behind glass doors. We knew nothing about what happened to them, for their newspapers, magazines and books spoke nothing of their life, their sorrows and joys. They repeated only what Peking told them to. The Shanghai *English Daily* reprinted day after day the editorials of Peking's *People's Daily*. People did not speak or approach a stranger and in spite of the public receptions and banquets, there was little warmth and much less of human relationships. From Peking to Canton we heard the same speeches of welcome, of peace and Asian unity, of American imperialists and of two thousand years' interflow of culture. There was no need to translate these speeches after a while, for we knew every word of them.

It was no different, basically, in the villages and in the rest of the country. Though the Communist revolution had begun in the countryside, and land reform had brought new hope in the rural areas, it could not create a sound agrarian economy. It gave the peasants a new sense of power, which they exercised through the Farmers' Associations. The women were liberated and new vitality abounded in the village. Now the peasants wanted to be left alone to till their lands and "grow rich," but the Communists could not leave them alone. Through propaganda, indoctrination and market control the peasant was slowly being regimented. The peasants of Kao Kang village in Manchuria were in obvious conflict with the collective spirit.

We went to the village of Küfow, to the tomb of Confucius. The "common good" in this little village did not appear to have cleaned away the dust of ages. The fields were ripe with corn but in the village there were dust and poverty. Broken-down huts lined the streets and the peasants moved across the fields bent under heavy burdens. Obviously it was not a village on show.

Mao, too, had come to this village and to the temple of Confucius, during his wanderings after his hungry years at the Peking University library. Here Confucius had lived and taught his *Analects* more than two thousand years ago. He left behind a permanent impression of his teachings on the life of the people. The code of filial piety, ancestor worship, the training in Confucian virtues, respect for wisdom and veneration of age, and the ritual of politeness, had all become part of the life of the nation. The people had accepted a code of social conduct but they had retained their individual private lives which asked only to be left alone as long as social obligations had been fulfilled. Only a free man could have written, as Po Chü-i did in the ninth century:

> Last year when I lay sick
> I vowed
> I'd never touch a drop again
> As long as I should live.
> But who could know
> Last year
> What this year's spring would bring?
> And here I am
> Coming from old Liu's home
> As drunk as I can be.

The old feudalism had been overthrown and its place is now taken by a dictator who rules in the name of the people. New China talks of democracy, but under communism there is little liberty for the individual. According to the Communists individualism leads to corruption, greed for power and bribery. The liberties the Common Program speaks of—freedom of speech, thought, publication, assembly, association, correspondence, person, domicile, religious belief and public demonstration—are only for the dictator. Freedom has been replaced by the "common good" and instead of personal rights there are obligations to "the people." And the people are commanded by the Communists. There is no liberty for the individual, for there is no rule of law.

No freedom of speech or association is possible when all publications and newspapers are required "not to violate the laws of the People's Government or disseminate propaganda injurious to the New Democracy." Opposition to the Common Program and the leadership of the Communist Party is treason. There is no source of news other than the government, and the Chinese newspapers are closed to any but the official views. No foreign news is published until the government releases it. Even Stalin's statement in reply to Ambassador Kirk was held back for days in October, 1951. I was in Nanking when Liaquat Ali, the ex-Prime Minister of Pakistan, was murdered. The Chinese newspapers contained no mention of it and we heard it only from one of the Indian Embassy officials. We wanted to listen to the Indian radio broadcast, but were told that no foreign broadcast could be received.

Literature is subordinated to politics and so are art, cinema and drama. All must serve the cause of the revolution. Once the Chinese Communists welcomed the foreign press and everything was open to public view. Today it is difficult to see anything or meet anyone; and even Mao, who drew his strength from his contacts with the people, has shut himself up behind the myth of the Saving Star. In spite of difficulties of language in many other countries I have visited, I had never felt so completely isolated.

There is no freedom of movement or domicile. People may not move from one district to another without a police permit, and a permit means long waiting, explanations and scrutiny. It was equally hard to leave China. The exit permit implied another long wait, possibly of months. For the lucky ones who get it, Shanghai night clubs play "He's a jolly good fellow" and celebrate. It is difficult to change residence for more than a day, and the change must be reported on the same day to the police.

Mao considered the building up of the People's Police as one of the main tasks of the revolution, for he needed the instrument of terror to unify the people. Thought control, self-criticism and brainwashing are conducted through education, propaganda, and district and street committees where wives are called upon to speak against their husbands, and children deem it their duty to inform against their parents. Groups of five have been formed to keep watch on one another, and the loyalty of each citizen is kept under surveillance.

The logic of totalitarian power has driven the Communist to organize periodic drives of liquidation. Concentration camps and suicides are the usual means which a dictatorship uses to instill fear and subjugate the people. Many friends of China have overlooked this recent development for they accept the sacrifices which revolution imposes. They point out that China's millions have at least obtained freedom from starvation and the women have been emancipated. It is temporarily true that the peasant's bowl of rice is fuller, that the women have found voice and new dignity, but how long will this satisfy the people, once life becomes constant slavery in the service of a dictatorship?

The Communists call China a New Democracy in which workers, peasants, the petty bourgeoisie and the national bourgeoisie are the "Four Friends" who enjoy all democratic freedoms under the leadership of the Communist Party. Many years ago, in *The New Democracy*, Mao wrote: "The New Democracy of a union of democratic classes is different in principle from a socialist state with the dictatorship of the proletariat. China, throughout the period of her new democratic system of government, cannot and should not have a system of government of the character of one-class dictatorship or one-party monopoly of government."

In proof of this attitude, it is asserted that the Chinese government today is a coalition government in which all the democratic parties which opposed the Kuomintang have a place. It is also pointed out that the membership of these parties is actively endorsed by the Communist Party itself.

I was in Peking when a series of articles appeared in the local press written by young men who wanted to join the Communist Party and had been directed to join other parties instead. The membership of the Communist Party today is more than five million, but with only two million proletariat in the country, the Party is overweighted with peasantry. It is an act of self-defense that the young recruits are directed to other parties. A Party member told me, "We are sending these recruits to other parties in order to help in the organization of these parties."

Mao has repeatedly written, "Our starting point is to serve the Chinese people earnestly and wholeheartedly and never to be severed from the people"; but the Communists have never attempted any analysis of the popular will and how it reveals itself. The "people's will" now expresses itself in the Fuehrer principle and the new mythology of China. The Common Program, the coalition and the New Democracy are based fundamentally on the leadership of the Communist Party and its head. All other classes must bow to the will of the proletariat and the groups in the coalition must accept that will as expressed by the Party.

Jack Belden writes, in *China Shakes the World*, "Mao's doctrine: 'Learn from the masses and then teach them' is a kind of perversion of Loyola's doctrine: 'Follow the other man's course to your own goal.' Thus, in the past, the Communists applauded the liberals, cheered the students, shouted for freedom of speech and abolition of tyranny." Now they shout for them still, but since the goal has been achieved freedom is to be given only to "the people" and not to the "reactionaries." A reactionary is today equated with anyone who opposes the dictatorship of the Communist Party.

Oh! You are the bright symbol and victorious flag,
Long live our venerable Mao Tse-tung.
We are fortunate to live in your era and learn your example.
We will follow you and enter a new world.

In the beginning the passion of the revolution had supplied the motive force to the state, and in the process men of different parties, politics and positions had acted jointly. Because the Communists utilized this passion, they succeeded in destroying the power of Chiang. Now the passion is stilled, and they find new limitations to their power.

There is a growing separation between the people and the Party. Hitherto the Communists had depended on their experience in the villages and the country. Today Mao lives in his secret temple and Liu Shao-chi doles out the theory of Maoism. In an attempt to explain it as a natural development of Leninism-Stalinism, China is drifting into a theoretical approach to her problems. Political and economic dependence and the hatreds of the past have driven the country into economic isolation.

The coalition government is in reality the government of the Communist Party. Other groups continue merely as a result of prior historical processes. How soon they will disappear depends more upon international developments than the conditions within the country. Mao has said: "Those who are with us will remain with us." Mme. Sun, virtually a prisoner of her own commitments to the Communists, remains only because she is Sun Yat-sen's wife.

Today, in four administrative areas out of six, there is military administration. The generals who administer these areas are old members of the Red Army. The People's Liberation Army, though not as homogeneous as in the past, has received special attention in the struggle. During the course of the last three years the army has been completely indoctrinated with the new beliefs, and the war in Korea was useful in its modernization.

Some have hinted at a possibility of conflict between the army and the Communist Party. They justify these views on grounds of the traditional history of China where the provincial ambitions of war lords have led to disintegration in the past. But the old Red Army is completely and wholly loyal to Chu Teh, and Chu Teh is devoted to Mao. Mao has also taken care to see that no army general is posted to an area in which he has any local influence.

The New Democracy is democracy only in name, and the coalition is only a façade. The people of China have no voice in the formation of policy. The mass is given the thrill of taking up the cry of the leader and thus participating in the execution of policy but the individual remains inchoate. He functions only as a model, as a cry-raiser.

THE GREAT PEACE

China is a totalitarian dictatorship in which the Communists are its temporal and spiritual rulers. They have humbled the ancient gods by making men's hopes appear capable of fulfillment in this life.

The new autocracy holds the daily life of the people at ransom. China is at peace. There is law and order within the country. And for millions of people on the land this is the great peace, the peace in which they can till the land they own and eat their daily bread. But soon the fruits of land reform will appear illusory as the pressure of the population operates upon it. The Communists' foreign policy has tied the country to a new imperialism which seeks to dominate not only men's lives but also men's minds. In the process a new slavery is being imposed on the millions of people. Inevitably, by its own logic, this so-called New Democracy is sowing the seeds of its own decay.

Mao once wrote a poem which embraces the whole of Chinese history:

> In this North country, in the flaming wind,
> A thousand acres are enclosed in ice,
> And ten thousand acres in whirling snow.
> Behold both sides of the Great Wall—
> There is only a vast desolation left.

China offers little hope for the future. Mao was a prophet of his own success. Will he be the doom of his failure?

Appendix

THE COMMON PROGRAM

On October 1, 1949, in the Tien An Man Square of Peking, Mao Tse-tung announced the founding of the People's Republic of China. "We, the 475 million Chinese, have now stood up and the future of our nation is one of unlimited brilliance." The government founded that day would, he said, "exercise the People's Democratic Dictatorship, in accordance with the Common Program, within the boundaries of the whole of China."

The Common Program is a document containing about sixty articles, together with the basic laws of the Chinese People's Political Consultative Conference and the Central People's Government. It was adopted at the first session of the People's Political Consultative Conference which was held in Peking from September 21 to 30, 1949. It was attended by 662 invited delegates representing various political parties and organizations of workers and peasants. In theory the Communist Party, as a party, is represented by the same number of members as ten other political parties in China, but representation was also given to the People's Liberation Army, the Communist-liberated areas and the so-called democratic organizations of students, women, youth and professions apart from the workers' and peasants' organizations. The admission of these groups gives the Communists more than a two-thirds majority of the seats, though in theory they hold only one-third.

The Chinese People's Political Consultative Conference (CPPCC) is supposed to act as a final legislature of the country, with powers to amend the organic laws or the Common Program, and to elect the National Committee until the All-Chinese People's Congress is elected and convened. The CPPCC is summoned to meet once every three years. Meanwhile, a smaller body called the National Committee of the CPPCC, carries on the functions allotted to it.

The National Committee is composed of 198 members elected from the CPPCC. It meets every six months under the auspices of its Standing Committee. The Standing Committee supervises the carrying-out of all the decisions of the National Committee in the interval between the plenary sessions of the CPPCC. The CPPCC has also a Central People's Government and an Administrative Council consisting of a chairman, six vice-chairmen and fifty-six council members. Under this Council there are at present five committees, twenty-one ministries, three commissions, four administrations and the People's Bank of China.

The Chairman of the Government is Mao Tse-tung. Six vice-chairmen serve under him, among whom are Chu Teh, Liu Shao-chi, Mme. Sun, Kao Kang and two others. The Administrative Council has Premier Chou En-lai and four vice-premiers and sixteen council members. Chou En-lai is also in charge of the Ministry of Foreign Affairs.

The five committees under the Administrative Council co-ordinate the work of several of the ministries. The Council of Financial and Economic Affairs, for example, co-ordinates the ministries of finance, trade, industries, agriculture and communications.

APPENDIX

The CPPCC also elects a Military Council, a Supreme Court, and the Procurator General's office. The Military Council is presided over by Mao as Chairman, six vice-chairmen including Chu Teh and two other generals, Chou En-lai, Liu Shao-chi and Kao Kang.

The country is divided into six administrative areas, four of which are run by a Military and Administrative Committee. Only the Northeast and the North have a People's Government.

The Common Program states in its preamble that the democratic dictatorship is "the state power of the People's democratic united front, composed of the working class, peasantry, petty bourgeoisie and national bourgeoisie." These are the "Four Friends." The Program calls upon the government to abolish all prerogatives, confiscate bureaucratic capital and carry out land reform. It further declares the objective of the state to be the "transformation of the country from an agricultural into an industrial one."

Article 6 of the Program says that the people of China shall have freedom of thought, speech, etc.

Article 8 imposes on every citizen an obligation to defend the fatherland, to abide by the laws, to observe discipline, protect public property, perform public and military services and to pay taxes.

Article 11 lays down the foreign policy. China is "to unite with all peace-loving and freedom-loving countries . . . first of all, the U.S.S.R."

The other sections of the Common Program deal with the organization of the state power. Economic policy is also described, and the laws of the Kuomintang are abolished.

Article 26 declares, "The basic principle of the People's Republic is to develop production through policies which take into account both the public and private interest and benefit both labor and capital." The state is called upon to co-ordinate the various sectors of the economy, organize factory administrative committees and lay the foundation for industrialization and socialism. The Program also assures other nationalities within China the protection of their culture and language, with a right to regional autonomy.

The last article accords asylum to "foreign nationals who seek refuge because they have been oppressed by their government for supporting the people's interests and taking part in the struggle for peace and democracy."

BIBLIOGRAPHY

Belden, Jack. *China Shakes the World*. Harper & Brothers, New York, 1949.

Bodde, Derk. *Peking Diary*. Henry Schuman, New York, 1950.

Chiang Kai-shek, General and Mme. *General Chiang Kai-shek*. Doubleday & Company, Inc., New York, 1937; with title *China at the Crossroads*. Faber & Faber, Ltd., London, 1937.

China Monthly Review, edited by John Powell. June, 1951– June, 1952.

China Reconstructs, an official quarterly published in Peking.

Chinese official publications, "The Common Program" and "Agrarian Reform Law."

Liu Shao-chi. (1) On the Party
               (2) On the Inner Party Struggle
               (3) How to Be a Good Communist
               (4) Internationalism and Nationalism

Mao Tse-tung (1) On a Prolonged War
              (2) The New Democracy
              (3) The Chinese Revolution and the Communist Party of China
              (4) Coalition Government
              (5) On People's Democratic Dictatorship
              (6) On Practice

Paul, Leslie. *Age of Terror*. Beacon Press, Boston, 1951.

Payne, Robert. *Mao Tse-tung*. Henry Schuman, New York, 1950.

Remer, C. F. *Foreign Investments in China*. The Macmillan Co., New York, 1939.

Snow, Edgar. *Red Star over China*. Random House, Inc., New York, 1937.

——*Battle for Asia*. Random House, Inc., New York, 1941.

Stein, Gunther. *The Challenge of Red China*. McGraw-Hill Book Company, Inc. New York, 1945.

Wales, Nym. *Inside Red China*. Doubleday & Company, Inc., New York, 1939.

Waley, Arthur. 170 *Chinese Poems*. Alfred A. Knopf, Inc., New York 1919.

——(editor). *China, Body and Soul*. Secker & Warburg, London, 1938.

Set in Linotype Janson
Format by Edwin H. Kaplin
Manufactured by The Haddon Craftsmen, Inc.
Published by HARPER & BROTHERS, *New York*